THE MESSENGER

Copyright © 2019 The Messenger.

All rights reserved. No part of this book may be reproduced, stored, or transmitted by any means—whether auditory, graphic, mechanical, or electronic—without written permission of the author, except in the case of brief excerpts used in critical articles and reviews. Unauthorized reproduction of any part of this work is illegal and is punishable by law.

The information, ideas, and suggestions in this book are not intended as a substitute for professional medical advice. Before following any suggestions contained in this book, you should consult your personal physician. Neither the author nor the publisher shall be liable or responsible for any loss or damage allegedly arising as a consequence of your use or application of any information or suggestions in this book.

ISBN: 978-1-4834-9623-8 (sc)
ISBN: 978-1-4834-9624-5 (e)

Library of Congress Control Number: 2019900518

Because of the dynamic nature of the Internet, any web addresses or links contained in this book may have changed since publication and may no longer be valid. The views expressed in this work are solely those of the author and do not necessarily reflect the views of the publisher, and the publisher hereby disclaims any responsibility for them.

Any people depicted in stock imagery provided by Getty Images are models, and such images are being used for illustrative purposes only. Certain stock imagery © Getty Images.

Lulu Publishing Services rev. date: 2/28/2019

Contents

Introduction vii
What God Doesn't Know 1
Is the World Your Oyster? 7
   Oyster Meditation 11
Perspective and Personality 13
   Perspective Meditation 15
Healing and Sicknesses 17
   Healing and Sickness Meditation 21
Big Bang 23
   Big Bang Meditation 26
Darkness of Mind 29
   Darkness of Mind (the Emptiness) Meditation 32
Fear 35
   Fear Meditation 40
Remembering and Forgetting 43
   Remembering and Forgetting Meditation 47
River of Life 49
   River of Life Meditation 52
Fact and Truth 53
   Fact vs. Truth Meditation 55
One Plus One Equals One 57
   One Plus One Meditation 60
First Time 63
   Meditation for the First-Time Experience 69
Searching vs. Seeking 71
   Searching vs. Seeking Meditation 74

Tree of Life...75
   Meditation for Tree of Life............................. 79
Inner Space..81
   Inner Space Meditation...................................85
Gratitude... 87
   Gratitude Meditation....................................93
Priorities...95
   Priorities Meditation...................................100
Time...103
   Time Meditation 108
Appendix..111
Glossary...119
Index..127

Introduction

How to Use the Book

The materials, or chapters, included here are not dependent upon each other. The best way to use this book is intuitively. Find a quiet place where you are not distracted. Then get mindful and read a page. Contemplate the message on this page. Then find the beginning of its chapter and read it in its entirety. Or you may also glance though the book and choose a title that appeals to you before reading it.

After finishing the chapter, let your mind juggle the information and sit with it for a while. At the end of almost every chapter is a meditation. In this book, we are not going to talk about the preparations or techniques of meditation. You can get these from any meditation handbook. Here we are talking about the essence of meditation. These are meditations through visualization. There are thousands of ways to meditate.

If we meditate long enough, then we can start to bring meditation into every aspect of our life. Then everything, that is, every activity of ours, becomes our meditation. All we need to do is to let go of our automatic pilot and bring some mindfulness to our activities. Basically meditation is a quality, and that quality is mindfulness. If you bring that mindfulness to any activity or anything that you are doing, then you are meditating.

Stop thinking that you need special or specific things like sitting and facing the east, reclining on a special cushion, or reciting a distinct mantra or that you cannot meditate because you are running out of incense. Of course, for the beginners, it is a great help to familiarize themselves with ceremonies and tranquility; however, we should also be careful that it not become a mindless pattern. Anything done automatically, that is, by routine, replaces mindfulness. If we are on automatic pilot, then we are away from meditation. Be careful that patterns and rituals don't replace the actual meditation.

Meditations that follow each chapter should be done in an upright spine position, if possible. Should your physical condition limit your sitting ability, as long as you are sincere and mindful, all meditations in this book can be done. Go through each meditation when you've finished reading the corresponding chapter.

After the initial meditation, you should do this same meditation every day for one to three weeks. While you are going through your daily activities, reflect back to your meditation and messages in its chapter. After the one- to three-week period, you may start another chapter, but you can always return to any of the previous chapters if you feel you need to go deeper.

You *can* meditate to music, but whether you use nature sounds like waterfalls, ocean waves, birds chirping, or insects buzzing or listen to other music, it should have no lyrics. Recited mantras are fine, something that doesn't need your attention when listening and flows easily for you. It should not take your attention away but help you to focus on the meditation.

What God Doesn't Know

I know you are curious and can't wait to read the final words to see *what God doesn't know*. And here is a promise: even after reading this short chapter, you will experience some of the glory, if not all of it, just as the universe has revealed it to this being. To follow this experience step by step, let's temporarily put aside our notion of individuality and tap into the truth that we are all one. From that noble place of this truth, what had been unleashed and showered on this being can be experienced again. So that there is no separation between us, let's put away the pronoun "I" for the entire book and instead use "the being."

Here is what happened: It was on a ferry ride one summer evening decades ago. The weather was unique, nothing like any weather the being had known before. It was not cold, windy, hot, or warm. It was just perfect (a reality that no imagination can follow). The waves around the ferry were dancing in a mysterious way so that thousands of shimmering reflections appeared and disappeared at the same time.

It was as if thousands of stars were born and collapsed almost at the same time. All this extraordinary beauty, art, and magic transformed and transcended the space and time. Suddenly the being was connected to what is called past, present, and future simultaneously. Time stopped and became eternal. Within the waves, the shimmering stars, and all this vastness of emptiness and eternity, the being thought, *Wouldn't God be afraid of this vastness?*

All these microscopic stars and galaxies transformed and transcended the being into macroscopic stars and galaxies. How long this out-of-body experience took, the being doesn't know, but eventually the being was returned to the ferry and could see itself in the physical body.

The gap might have been a brief moment or much longer. Decades after, the being even tries to comprehend what happened on that ride, but no explanation can match the experience. Possibly the question that arose was rhetorical … or even an answer.

Questions are shallow, while answers are deep and rooted. Questions may appear or disappear, but the answers will always be there. The quality within that brief moment brought something worthwhile to embrace with our whole being. Before we open that gap deeper, let us consider these two possibilities about all readers:

- You are a believer and believe in God.
- You are an atheist who doesn't believe in God.

If you are a believer who believes in God, you should know that different religions and sects have different views of God. That's why they have various ways to connect to "their" God. As we can see, the way that we worship in different religions, sects, or belief systems is partially or totally different. We reach for God in different ways—singing, dancing, chanting, or even beating ourselves and crying. So there are countless approaches and belief systems for the same name, God.

Even if we have the same religion as someone else, does it mean that we have the same God? We were introduced to God as children. Most likely this happened first through our families when we noticed our parents were talking about God. It doesn't matter whom we asked—our moms, dads, grannies, religious leaders, teachers, or daycare people. The answer was always the same. None of these people could show us God. Their descriptions of God were abstract and imaginary, including what they'd heard from their parents or grandparents.

Because none of these explanations were lucid expositions on God, we had to go to our own creation by the illusory mind. As humankind, we can talk about anything—any story and any kind of fantasy—and we can deliver thousands of facts or stories to others, but we can never transmit our imagination to others, so we had to create God in our own image. The subtler our consciousness, the subtler world we entered for that image.

All wars in human history in the name of religion or belief systems happen because of this mind mistake. In our own image, we created a god, and we claimed it as being *the* God. Whoever has imagined another god became our enemy.

We shout, "Are you blind? This is the only way to go to God!"

We forget that the conceptualized reality is only the construct of our own minds. If we are in desperate need, our prayers become begging. If we are sick, we imagine God as a healer. If we need strength, God appears as a hero. Because mostly we think materialistically, we attach God to some worldly object or event. Because we have appeared as human beings and we have physical appearances, feelings, and emotions, we bring all these factors to the image of God.

On the other hand, if you are an atheist the God that others have created in their own image doesn't resonate with you. You realize that every individual is unique and should follow their own unique path to the highest frequency in the universe. Unfortunately, there is a common misunderstanding about atheists. The view is that if you are an atheist you are misled, and have lost the connection to higher self and existence. The challenge between the believer and atheist is created mostly because of words like: judgement, ownership, God, ad infinitum. Most likely, both groups shall find the same foundation if they let go of their own creation and dogma and open their horizon towards the true nature of the phenomena that is based on the highest cosmic vibration and frequency.

That's why during the spiritual experience on the ferry ride, the being thought, *Wouldn't God have fear?*

That thought was followed by the recognition that fear exists only in the physical world: fear of losing something or fear of decline.

Living in the world, we know everything has its own lifetime. Things, if they don't break, get old and return to the departure line. A human's life is no exception. That's why any sense of possession of anything attaches to its corresponding sense of fear: fear of deterioration or fear of departure.

But in the spirit realm, there is no physicality of anything to undergo the law of entropy. The dichotomy is that humans have one foot in each realm. The physical body must go through the law of entropy, while the spirit stays an entity of the spirit realm. We forget that we are spirits. We have temporary physical bodies in order to experience human life on a beautiful planet.

Some of us only live in the external world and never go on a deep journey inside of us to discover everything that is available to us. We use only our five senses (sight, hearing, smell, taste, and touch) to operate daily in life. Because we are spirit, we always have this yearning and longing for spiritual nourishment; therefore, we are always searching deep inside. The God that we are introduced to is only a super figure. The God that is created in the human image is a superhero but has some human qualities, such as anger and fear.

Hey, friends, the emotions of fear, anger, and jealousy are human attributes. If we have conceptualized or created a god with these attributes, we had better start reconstruction and recreation immediately.

Rumi said, "There is no name, no color, no shape to God. If we have created a god with a name and shape, we have created something that stops us from realizing God."

If we think that God has created all the stars and galaxies and the entire cosmos, then it should be impossible to imagine a god that is jealous. We always think that the reason for our anger remains in the external world, but anger is a reflection of our inner world. We get angry because some thing or circumstance triggers or unleashes the poison inside us.

Should we imagine a compassionate and loving God who gets angry? Whenever we are insecure, weak, or shaky or when we are grasping in order not to lose something, we develop fear. Therefore, an image of a fearful god is not correct.

God knows no fear. Of course, God knows about *our* fear, but God doesn't know fear as an experience. God knows about existing hate in so many different realms, but God doesn't know the feeling or emotion or ever experiences a stroke of hate.

The ferry reached its destination. The being stood on the deck of the ferry and realized that something had changed. Everything was more beautiful and more loving: the people, water, clouds, sky, and even the cars. Everything felt closer and more intimate, as if the external world had entered and become inner space. The being realized the familiar image of God had left, but everyone and everything had become another face of God, as if all existence had become the image of God.

The being realized that a major shift had happened inside, like a caterpillar in a chrysalis goes through a metamorphosis, changes to a butterfly, and suddenly is able to fly above the tree that was holding space for it. A new being had given rise to the previous one, the one who took the ferry ride. It was as if that ride had gifted a pair of glasses through which the being was able to see life differently, now much brighter and more colorful.

The new being could finally understand the true meaning of the words such as *compassion, kindness, gentleness,* and *love.* All became alive and could all travel much farther and deeper and make more sense than words such as *anger, frustration, hate,* and *fear.*

The being got a new translator that translated every single word differently. For the old being, words were most likely only definitions that were lodged in the mind. They had no opportunity to be more than their definitions. And for the new being, words became organic and flexible and had the ability to swim in different currents in the mind.

One big difference between the old and new being was the sense of ownership. The new being realized that the greatest obstacle between the divinity of God and individuals is the sense of ownership. The illusion of ownership has merged into our being so deeply that, not only do we think we own objects such as cars and properties, we think we also own people. We own not only our friends but also our children or spouses.

We have exercised the illusion of ownership so often that we think even God belongs to us and we are the only ones who have *the* God. We forget that the indivisible and infinite ocean of the power and bliss, God, cannot be owned by anyone. We think the god that others believe in is not *the* God, that is, that theirs is just a god.

Any sense of ownership is another distraction that takes us away from divine eternity and infinitude and captures and freezes us in some material object or the illusion of power. We get frozen in an illusionary time-space loop. The new being understood that only having a spiritual experience is not enough to realize the truth and the actual earth work had begun. Knowing that the divinity of God cannot be understood or shown to anyone and that the reality of that truth can only be realized, attained, and eventually lived, the new being took a vow to deliver that spiritual experience to as many other beings as possible. The book that you are reading is the result.

Is the World Your Oyster?

Is the world your oyster, or are you the oyster of the world? If you are the oyster of the world, it depends on how you operate in this moment. How you operate now depends on your reality that you have created in the past. If you have only seen the glass half empty, that is how you see the world right now. If you have the determinant's attitude or the fatalist's behavior or have a tendency toward pessimism, then you are the oyster because things have been decided for you. You are only fulfilling the scripture that was handed in at the time of your birth. It's only a matter of time that you fulfill your role. If you are a fatalist, then there is no room in your awareness for any radical change or changes.

For example, imagine you are John. You are an employee of a company. You like golf, but you dislike all other sports. You'd like to meet a nice girl and to enjoy her companionship, but you don't know where to meet her. The two female coworkers are already engaged in relationship, and because you are always shy, not an outgoing character, you are not going out of your house for evening activities. Instead you are watching TV throughout the afternoon and night. You are pretty much bored with your life; however, there is no way to change it unless one day good luck comes and knocks at your door and the change of your lifestyle is brought to you.

But how do you define good luck? Why is John not getting up, going out, or creating his fun? Doesn't he know about his freedom? Doesn't he know about human's free will? Just one thing, fear, stops all the process of life. Fear of the unknown stops John from taking action. Out of his fear, John, you, and I choose all kinds of determinist attitudes.

John is afraid to be free because freedom is risky. And John is afraid because his mind, which holds his makeup, all of his upbringing, and training, is with him. The imposed fear of mother, grandmother, and families is within his mind. Of course, John is afraid of his mind, which has the agent of society within him—the society that shows him the half-empty glass and translates common sense, compassion, and love into duties and obligations.

A suggestion is to erase words like *duties* and *obligations* out of your mind's dictionary and replace them with heart words like *compassion* and *love*. Humans have two very powerful laws that govern their lives. Everybody knows about the law of gravitation, the life force that pulls everything downward, but very few people in the world know about the law of levitation. This life force pulls everything upward.

When we have the half-empty-glass mentality, it's like only being aware of the law of gravity, and that is the duty and obligation kind of person. On the other hand, when we have the half-full-glass mentality, the upward-pulling levitation—which some masters call love, grace of god, grace, or god—we have an embracing personality.

Just a few yogis here and there are using the levitation energy. Some of us have never thought about it, and many of us have never heard about it. We believe in the magical power of Rambo, Rocky, and Arnold. That is Hollywood made, but we don't believe in the magical, alchemical, divine power levitation. Let us see where it all started.

It all started in the family. When we hear "these are your duties" from our parents, we divide the world into "their obligations" and "our duties." We start to think that our parents are doing their job—that they are fulfilling their duties or are obligated. But parents know deep inside that they are doing all this because of their (unconditional) love.

We don't need to be cute or even sweet in order for our parents to take care of us. They just took responsibility because of their love, not due to a duty or obligation. Love doesn't have any duties or know any responsibility. Love is unconditional and our natural state. We don't need to practice it. We need only to reveal it. Just be natural and let the love flow.

Was all of creation based on love or obligation? Do the trees have any duties to provide branches for the birds? Or is it the duty of the insect to carry pollen from flower to flower for fertilizing? When we talk about duties and obligation, we also create punishment because we feel we have come up short in the fulfillment of our so-called duties. The punishment might be the penalty we pay by way of a traffic ticket that you pay at court or the guilt we feel when we are at the court of our belief system.

The difference between the concept of responsibility and obligation is tricky. We willingly take on challenges and tasks and make them our responsibility because of love, like holy beings, who out of love and compassion for other humans, willingly take on responsibilities. For example, Mother Theresa cared for so many orphans in India and didn't see this service as a duty. She *took* the responsibility because of her love and compassion.

No one can give us a responsibility. We must take it upon ourselves out of love. Society uses the word *responsibility* incorrectly. It is in our vocabulary now as an obligation, something pushed on us by another or a duty given to us from the outside, not something we do out of love. A child given the task of taking out the garbage fulfills that duty because of the obligation his or her parent has given him, not necessarily out of love. His or her incentive might be rewards or a fear of his or her parents, but it's not because he or she loves to take out the garbage.

John wants to go out and to have some fun. He hears his mom's voice in his head, "You are responsible for your actions."

Poor John thinks, *If I go out and something bad happens, I can't blame my coworkers for that or push the fault onto my neighbors.*

Why should John take risks and jump into the unknown when he can sit in his room and watch TV? He's familiar with his boredom, and he doesn't see that freedom from his boredom is in the unknown. Poor John doesn't know that love, not obligation, took care of him as a child. He doesn't know that words have tremendous power. Because of the misuse of the words, John is confused.

If you are a good parent, you think you are obligated to your baby's life, right? And one may say, "Of course I'm obligated. Who else would take care of my children?"

Does it mean that you didn't fulfill your responsibility or were short in duty when your baby gets sick? Does it mean that our universal parents, our god, is also responsible for you and your baby? Does it mean that God failed while you were sick or miserable?"

Friends, God is not a loveless dictator, a psycho-general, an aggressive officer, or any kind of unhuman authority. Words like *hate, anger, jealousy,* and *duties* as well as twisted responsibility come from other entities. Just look at how many words of military or authorities have spread into our daily language. If we have an appointment with someone at four o'clock, instead of saying, "Let us send an intention to meet at four o'clock," we say, "Let's *shoot* for four o'clock."

When we have some extra time before four o'clock, instead of saying "Shall we embrace the extra gift of time?" we say, "Let's kill the time." Job and work come in every other sentence.

- Instead of saying "brave," "great," or "well done," we reply "good job" or "nice work."
- Instead of training the body and exercising, using our energy and strength, we say "*work*out."
- Instead of saying "to digest" or "to get insight for something," we say "we have *work* to do."
- Instead of saying "we are solving a misunderstanding," we say "*work* it out."
- Instead of saying "to get rid of something," we say "*work* it off."
- When we want to include something, we say "*work* it in."
- When we describe the particular subject in which a group of people share an interest, we say "*work*shop."

Now that we have the definitions of responsibility and obligation and see the differences between embracing or killing time, let us use the words correctly.

Oyster Meditation

Sit quietly in a comfortable place where you are not distracted by anyone or outside circumstances, like ringing phones. Make sure you feel comfortable enough to sit for a while without changing your position, and contemplate.

> Am I the oyster of the world? Am I living in poverty, meaning "there is no solution to my challenges or so-called problems"? Am I living in the reality of the half-empty-glass attitude? Am I using the free will gifted to me, or is it still deposited in my being like a savings account? Do I want to change the current reality to a domain of divine grace?

Sit long enough so the feeling of being the oyster of the world disappears and the wish to be free and not tagged or angled by the world rises within you. Once that wish arises, single-mindedly meditate on that wish for some time.

Rise out of the meditation and water that wish plant during the day and whenever you remember that wish.

Perspective and Personality

Most of our strengths or weaknesses are in our imaginations or only in our mind. If you get a pimple at the corner of your nose, it is in a place that is not easy for anyone else to see at first glance, and someone must really investigate your nose closely in order to find it. If we start to focus on that little pimple every time we look at the mirror, to remind our self about it, we might even forget to see our face. Eventually in our mind we'll create a blemish that is much bigger and fuller, one that everyone will see at first glance even before he or she sees our face.

Our strengths or weaknesses are mainly our mind's creation. They are only our own reality and not the Truth. Because they are our creations, they are different for everyone. We try to emphasize our strengths and hide our weaknesses. If the weaknesses are so obvious that they are not easily hidden, we start to create a powerful strength that becomes our dominant reality/personality.

Now we think we are safe again because we can hide our self behind that strength. That strength for many is money. They can hide themselves behind money, houses, or luxury cars. Some people become such compulsive shoppers that they cannot wear the same dress or piece of clothing twice. They constantly have to have something new in order to be able to hide themselves behind it. When such people are in a social gathering, they play the game of competition and comparison. If they have an expensive luxury car and if they are in a gathering with a few other people, they review in their mind what kind of car each one has so that in their mind they receive the higher placing.

They will not, for example, compare who has the best recipe for a delicious meal, got the best time in a race, has the best yoga posture, penned the best poem, or has the best singing voice. There would be no comparison unless they could collect the most credit. One other weakness protection is the creation of status. Adding a title to the beginning or end of a name, such as doctor or professor, allows the person with the weakness to hide behind the title.

For example, Doctor Mike will never again only be Mike. All of these comparisons and competitions are made because we are living in our intellectual mind. This is the mind that creates good and bad, and because of that creation, we have to constantly compare ourselves with other people in order to get a higher place or ranking for the sake of our ego. If we drop our ego, then we don't need to compare ourselves with others. And if we drop the comparison, the created weakness will disappear also. Then there is no need for hiding behind the imaginary strength. We see that they are all connected like a chain and one link depends on the next one.

Cutting though the chain is not easy, but again the good news is that it is a chain. If we cut through the right element, we could be free from the whole chain. Masters give us tools to cut though that chain. One tool is to cultivate the mind of gratitude.[1] With the mind of gratitude, many advanced disciples cut though the chain. This mind just appreciates not only whatever reality we are living in now but also whatever comes.

---

[1] See the chapter on gratitude.

Perspective Meditation

Sit quietly in a comfortable place, where you can be for a while and not be distracted. In addition to your quiet place, you will also need a vase with cut flowers or a potted plant that is blooming. Place the plant or vase of flowers on a table at eye level to where you are sitting, and contemplate.

> The way I view life depends on the angles, perspective, and my personality. I am that view to my reality and think it is *the* reality. I am going through this meditation to experience this truth: by changing my perspective, that is, altering the view of the observer, the observed is also transformed.

Now focus your attention on the view of the flowers you have at this angle. Look closely and go through as many details as you can before changing your position around the table.

At the new position and new angle, it looks like a new plant. Familiarize yourself with the new position and perspective before you move again. Move to at least seven different positions and perspectives around the table to be able to experience. By changing the observer's view, the observed is changed.

Coming back to the first starting point, look at the plant and notice that you have moved 360 degrees around the flowers. But you positioned yourself only seven times. Yet there are many, many more views than just the seven stops you made around the flowers.

Notice that you have moved around the plant in a complete circle, but only positioned yourself seven times. You could have taken 360 different positions, one degree for every position. Furthermore, there are infinite circles that you can draw around the plant, so we have countless possibilities to view that plant. From some of the positions, for example, the circle below the plant, from that view, we would see no flowers or plant when we are underneath the table.

Healing and Sicknesses

Let us contemplate some of the most human-hunted questions about healing. Why are some people sick almost all the time and others are almost never ill? Are the people who get sick more often exposed longer or more intensely to the virus and germs?

A friend once told me, "I have a bad pain in my lower back, and sometimes it's better, and other times it's worse. My dad has the same thing, and his father had suffered from the same pain his whole life."

Essentially the symptoms run in the whole family. Can a condition like this run through a generation? If so, where is this information stored? In so-called DNA strands? If so, would it be possible to change that kind of information? And if we want to bring some healing to the sicknesses, where shall we start?

Both healing and sickness are energy. Healing energy is sweet, soothing, and very desirable, and sickness energy is not. In order to understand the case of healing a sickness, we need to deepen our understanding about energy. Energy or Qi (pronounced "chi or key") is so big that we need to divide it into branches and sometimes localize it to give it a definition. Basically, we can say there is visible and invisible Qi or energy.

For example, we cannot see the energy of intention or will, but eventually we observe the manifestation of that kind of invisible energy. By the same token, we don't see the invisible energy of love, but we feel the sudden running of hot honey all over us. The most powerful energy in the universe, the energy of faith, isn't visible, but it can move the heaviest objects, for example, when there's a need to save a life or perform a good deed. In energy healing, we are exposed to the higher and/or the highest frequencies of cosmic energy, pranic and spiritual. Both of these invisible energies can be manifested and observed through energy healing.

There was once a firekeeper who explained the term of energy so beautifully. He made a holy fire for a ceremony. The holy fire was made in its original way, which meant no matches or gas lighter was used. The fire was made as our caveman ancestors did, using some fine shavings (carved wood), little twigs and branches, and flint. Two flints were rubbed against each other to make sparks, which randomly spread out from the flints. The carved wood (the bedding) was then held close to the flints to catch a spark.

Once the spark was on the bedding, the firekeeper blew on the spark, and the mixture of air and spark eventually grew into a little fire. The little fire would be fed by bigger and bigger pieces of wood until the fire got strong and solid.

Once the firekeeper made the fire as we described above, he asked, "Was the energy of the fire in the flints or the bedding? Or was it the air blown into it or in the wood added to the fire?" After that he explained the invisible and unformed energy of fire was formed and manifested in the flints that were rubbed against each other.

The energy hidden in the one spark has the potential to create a big fire; however, that energy should be guided to the right environmental conditions, to the dry tinder in the bedding. Fire is the only element that contains both formed and unformed energy. The flames of a fire appear and disappear.

So now let us compare this understanding of fire energy with the energy of sicknesses. Viruses and germs are living inside and outside each of us and all the time. For example, human beings usually get the flu in wintertime. However, there are people who get the flu in all seasons. We know people who get it once, twice, or more in a year, while a few other people hardly ever get the flu.

The energy of sickness, in this case, the flu, is in the flu virus, like the energy of the fire is in the flints. But this energy needs the right environment to grow into the flu. A person with a weak immune system has the right conditions for flu. An individual with a strong immune system may be exposed to lots of flu viruses but not get sick.

What are the requirements for a strong immune system? The answer is a heathy diet with enough vitamins, minerals, and lots of physical exercise. But the biggest component of a healthy, strong immunity is our belief system that manifests itself in the form of attitude, behavior, and necessary environmental adjustments and adaptation.

The good news is that the relationship between our inner being or our belief system and our external appearance such as our physical body and the external world is a two-way street. A person with low self-esteem may take lots of vitamins and minerals, but he or she is not encouraged in physical exercise and training. This individual engages in little or no activities.

If we have a fun, humorous personality, we will laugh easily. But even if we don't have an outgoing personality and we put on a smile or laugh, the happy and joyous endorphins are released in the body, and the messages of lightness change our mood and mind-set. The emotional burdens get lighter or disappear entirely. That healing medicine of humor and laughter has been used in yoga for centuries.

What happens when we engage in laughter-yoga? Not only do we release muscle tension, which automatically reduces pain, we also improve the blood circulation, which increases the oxygenation of blood, producing more energy. Anxiety and stress reduction is another benefit in laughter-yoga because it is almost impossible to keep our muscle tension and maintain our stress level while we are laughing.

Stress energy is dense and congested. With humor and laughter, that stuck, dense energy starts to ripple and flow again. Here is the crowning glory: the improvement and strengthening of the immune system because of laughter's effect on the neuroendocrine and stress hormones.

The actual act of laughing is not the only thing to change the biochemistry in our body, but through face-yoga, the very act of silently lifting the corners of our mouth and putting a smile on our face gives us the same benefits. We don't need to be a yogi or attend special classes to be able to do these healing exercises. We can do it at home or at work.

Not only is putting a smile on our face going to change our body chemistry, it also makes our coworkers, or whomever we encounter, feel better. The only problem in using this powerful free medicine remains in our misunderstanding about laughter. We think we need to be engaged in some kind of external humorous situation or observing a funny scene in order to be allowed to laugh.

You may think the reason of our laughter was a joke someone told us. If a joke is the true reason for our laughter, everyone who will hear it would start to laugh. But if we tell the same joke to many different people, we'll see a variety of reactions. Some may smile and chuckle; others may laugh genuinely or loud. A few may roll on the floor with tears of joy in their eyes. Some may be humiliated and even angry. They're all responding to the same joke. The same is valid for the funny scene or humorous situation.

The reason for our laughter doesn't lie outside of us and is not coming from outside in, but travels from inside out. The true reason for our laughter is our own humor. A joke or a funny scene may trigger the release of our response, but they are not the actual cause. Understanding that truth, we are all entitled to the healing energy of laughter. It makes us a good member of the universal health club. There are many documented cases of this healing medicine. For example, Norman Cousin's book, *The Anatomy of an Illness*, reports how he escaped the trip down with cancer and changed the direction with the powerful healing medicine of laughter.

Many masters encourage us to have at least a dose of ten minutes of laughter every morning after our sleeping journey, prior to getting out of bed and before we get involved in the seriousness of the world. The healing of this powerful medicine has the power to carry us through the day and beyond.

Healing and Sickness Meditation

Sit quietly in a comfortable position. Find your breath, and breathe deeper and slower. With each breath, notice how your mind becomes more quiet and peaceful. Remind yourself:

> I am sitting here to transcend any or all of my sicknesses. (We don't want to fall into the trap of all the details; we just want to remember the main causes of illness.) I am also sending my sincere intention for the blessing and healing, as a request to the Great Spirit.

Sit as long as you need until you start to feel or reach the higher frequencies[2] of the cosmic energy. You may enjoy this ecstasy as long as you wish before rising out of the meditation.

---

[2] By transcending sickness and receiving healing energy (energy healing), we are exposed to the higher and/or the highest frequencies of the cosmic energy, pranic and spiritual. Both of these invisible energies can get manifested and be observed through energy healing.

Big Bang

The common understanding of the big bang, the creation and expansion of the physical universe, is only a part of the original big bang. Masters who have spent a long time in deep meditation capturing messages about creation report of a magical spark that not only allows the manifested universe to *be* but also eventually carries it back to the un-manifested, pure consciousness.

Way back through to the creation while the pure consciousness was transforming itself to the physical universe, part of this transparent pure consciousness stayed unmanifested in the physical universe. The best way to understand this is to look at the human creation. Imagine an old, traditional scale with a long bar and two dishes hanging from chains at each end. On one side is pure consciousness; on the other side is the pure consciousness transformed into the physical body, thoughts, emotions, and mind. A magical spark of pure consciousness continued to exist unmanifested in all these four phenomena. The grace and blessings of this pure consciousness in these four phenomena result in:

- The ability for the physical body to heal itself
- The emotional body to create art and music
- The ability to think
- The mind's ability to analyze and discover

Unfortunately, we forgot about this magical spark inside of us, and we emphasized only our form and manifested consciousness.

Every Olympic Games, we observe that the athletes who have focused on that magical spark and trained enough break some previous records, but none of the credit goes to the right place. None of these new records are attributed to that powerful and magical unmanifested consciousness within the human race. Instead all credit is given to some individuals.

Mostly those individuals get lost in a particular flag, or a country. At the end of every Olympic Games, there would only be a list of countries and how many medals each one has collected. And the end credit goes to the commercial industry and politics. The magical spark, the true hero behind all the medals collectively, doesn't get any recognition. It stays unseen and unnoticeable.

It doesn't matter where we are born and which culture we grown up in. We are all trained to think materialistically and emphasize and value our physical identities. Deep inside, the origin of every form is spirit. To stay only in the form, without recognizing the spirit, the form only by itself is incomplete. That's why every form that we take we feel incomplete. We feel we are missing something; therefore, we search for that something to add to our broken or incomplete self in order to become complete. We use all our resources, intelligence, and talent and time to reach that piece or the pieces we need in order to become whole. We buy material things such as jewelry, cars, and houses. We go shopping as much as we can, and we are always searching. We ask about new shopping centers or more fancy things and are always waiting for something or someone to cross our path.

Meanwhile we pretend that we are complete and we have found what we have been searching for. We put on a mask in order to cover our incompletion. We live our entire life underneath this mask. We live that way so others have no access to see beneath the mask, but we ourselves have no desire to look underneath the mask. As time passes, we have less interest and desire to look into our self underneath the mask. The more roles played by this pretending delusional self, the less courage we have, and the slimmer the chance we have to look behind the veils.

The bad news is, while we write the perfect scenarios to play, life is not waiting for our scenarios to be acted. Life continues to flow. The organic and alive moments that were available to use to experience life have passed away. Now the acting comes. Many things that were not included in our thoughts and plans appear. Suddenly we feel new incompletion in the form of anger, sorrow, fear, and hate. And other delusions are added to our collection. Now we need even more thoughts and time as well as new ways to repair or replace things in order to move in the directions of completion. We never understand that the nature of any form is incompletion. Therefore, it doesn't matter how many eons we try in the form dimension, we shall not find completion. We think there are good days and there are bad days. Tomorrow it will be different, or there would be many, many situations in the journey.

For example, this station was not good, and I could not get what I needed. So I shall reach it in another station. We don't recognize that it is not the problem of the stations on the way, which delusions create, but it is the wrong direction.

We don't comprehend that, by changing the direction from going into the world of objects and forms and walking toward spirit and allowing consciousness to become aware of itself, the delusions will disappear. When we are walking away from the sun, we shall see our shadows. Once we change the direction and walk toward the sun, suddenly all the shadows disappear.

While walking away from the sun, we see shadows, but we also see indirect sunshine. By turning toward the sun, not only do the shadows disappear, we also get to see the source. While we are searching in the form dimensions, we have our consciousness, but it's not aware of itself (like indirect sunshine). By turning toward the sun, we see the direct sunshine and the awareness that is becoming aware of itself. Finding the source of the light is finding our true self.

Big Bang Meditation

Sit in a comfortable position, where you are not distracted with external circumstances, and contemplate:

> My whole being is the combination of many things formed and unformed as well as manifested and unmanifested. If I am going back to a solid imagination of myself again and again, grasping it, cherishing it, and making it a reality, it doesn't mean that I am who I am thinking I am. The range of being (ROB) is the vastness of creation itself. Any being in the form consciousness as a human being is that vastness. Where the awareness goes, the intention and attention follow. I am sitting here to get an experience of that truth.

Find your breath, and follow the breath. If you are breathing in, then breathe in moment by moment by moment. If you are exhaling, follow the breath moment by moment by moment. Get deeper and slower with each breath. Enjoy your breath as long as you wish before bringing your attention to the body and scan through the following:

- Neck and head
- Chest and belly
- Right arm, forearm, and hand
- Left arm, forearm, and hand
- Right leg and foot
- Left leg and foot

Now bring your awareness to the place you are sitting, and feel the border between you and the place you are sitting. Bring your attention to the environment where you are sitting. (If you are in a garden or an open field, listen to the birds singing or flapping their wings. If you are on a beach, listen to the waves. If you are listening to meditation music, bring your attention to the music.)

Send your awareness to the center of Mother Earth. See how the boiling, life-giving magma is giving birth to itself. Feel the warmth and power. Stay there as long as you wish before moving back to your breath, where you started.

As you felt, wherever your attention goes, it becomes your reality. While the awareness is down in the center of the earth, we have no record of the body or even pain we may have felt when our attention was focused on the body. It's the same way when the attention is with the singing birds, ocean waves, or music. We were not even feeling where we were sitting.

Focus on the truth of that experience you have received through this meditation, and sit with it for a while before your rise out of the meditation.

Darkness of Mind

Once a little boy ran to his father because he was afraid of darkness and couldn't sleep.

The father came with a flashlight into his room, saying, "We need to catch the darkness and throw it out. First, we need to investigate the darkness, little by little, corner by corner. And it doesn't matter how long it will take. We will stay awake and not fall asleep while we are investigating."

Both lost some of their valuable sleeping time, but the boy learned two profound wisdoms:

1. We cannot throw out or bring in the darkness.
2. Darkness is weightless and shapeless. That's why we cannot catch it.

Later on in life, the boy was afraid of his own darkness, and his venerable father gave him another flashlight, but this time the flashlight was called meditation. And this time, the darkness was his thoughts. In meditation, the light of wisdom gets through all the darkness of thoughts. It goes through all the thoughts within that make us insecure, uncomfortable, doubtful, or fearful. We try to throw out the darkness by bringing in more pleasure. We go to a movie, watch TV, go shopping, attend a party, or visit friends. Guess what? These all will bring more thoughts and more confusion.

Darkness is the absence of light; thoughts are the absence of meditation. When we are full of thoughts, which is not unusual in modern life, we don't need to put more thoughts on top of them. But because we are living in a consumer society, the natural process would be "get more" or "get bigger." We don't come to the conclusion to empty ourselves first.

Every house is full of stuff everywhere—in the living room, dining room, bedroom, and kitchen. Especially all the closets are full. Not only are they full, they get fuller and fuller. That's why we need storage units. But now even the storage units are too full. We've never learned that, before we add more, first we need to empty. If we start to empty the closet, we'll notice articles of clothing we've never used.

There are families that, after cleaning the stuff out of the closet, everything goes back in again, and the stuff never gets used until the next time they decide to clean it out. Have you ever tried to go for a short trip for a weekend in a cabin by the sea or camping in the woods, to live for a few days with only a couple of things? It's amazing how little we need. Consuming is a one-way street, which only knows "buy more," "get more," and "take in more."

Once I promised to help a grandma carry an antique armchair to her storage unit. When she opened the unit's door, things fell out, and I almost got injured. Barely peeking into the space, we found boxes and boxes in various conditions, along with chairs and tables piled on top of one another. It was a huge mess.

With little hope, I looked at her and said, "First, something that you really don't need and don't use must come out of there. Maybe go to a charity? Can you think of something?"

She said, "I haven't been here in years, and as a matter of fact, I don't even know what's in there."

When we observe the nature of a human being, we notice a kind of peeling away of processes. This process is nonstop, like the way we lose skin cells and our hair, consume water and urinate, or consume and process food and then eliminate wastes. Imagine what would happen if we only took in food without processing or eliminating it. That's the way the grandma was operating, to only take in stuff for years.

Meditation is cleansing. It's taking away all the thoughts that are not needed. Maybe some thoughts will persist, but with regular meditation, they will also fall away. Because through its peeling-away process of thoughts, all of our wishes, expectations, disappointments, and plans fall away too. The purpose of this peeling-away process is the total cleaning of the house, and when we one day face the empty house and nothing is left to throw away, we have reached enlightenment. This will only happen when we take off the mind's clothes and, one by one, empty all the closets.

Our mind can never enter the stage naked. It always has to disguise itself. It always has another costume, according to what the play is. If we remove all the clothing and masks away from the closet of the mind, nothing will be left over, and we recognize that the mind had power over us because of all the different clothes that we were keeping in the mind's closet. We were the ones who were holding space for all the performances of the mind.

Let us decide right now to empty some of the mind's closets and throw out what keeps us hostage. The follow is a basic emptiness meditation. Not only is it effective for one single use, it is worthwhile to employ in everyday life and before reading any chapter so you may empty your mind to make room for the new.

Darkness of Mind (the Emptiness) Meditation

Find a quiet place where you can be for a while without any external distraction, where there is no phone and no music.

Find your breath, and start to breathe deeper. Notice how your slow breathing is quieting your mind, and continue to breathe slower and deeper until your mind becomes contented. Now breathe deep and slow without any thought or image. Even let go of your breath. (Don't worry. The body's intelligence will continue to breathe for you without you focusing on your breath.)

Now see the sky, a sky without anything—no clouds, no birds, and no sun. There is only your mindfulness and the empty sky. There is only your mindfulness and the vastness.

Sit long enough that your mindfulness and vastness become one. Be in that vastness until a sense of manifestation of being "you" appears again. That usually happens if the physical body needs to change its sitting position.

A Note to the Beginners

We might not get to the vastness if we are beginners, but there is a promise here that at least you shall get the expansion. Every time that you do this meditation, some or many thoughts that have been hunting you shall disappear. The way that our mind works is through images and stories. Even when we are sitting for meditation, we still have an image of our self. That's why we are not truly meditating. We practice to reach a level where we are able to meditate. The emptiness or vastness meditation will train you to expand enough so you can meditate. Again, the key to all this is practice.

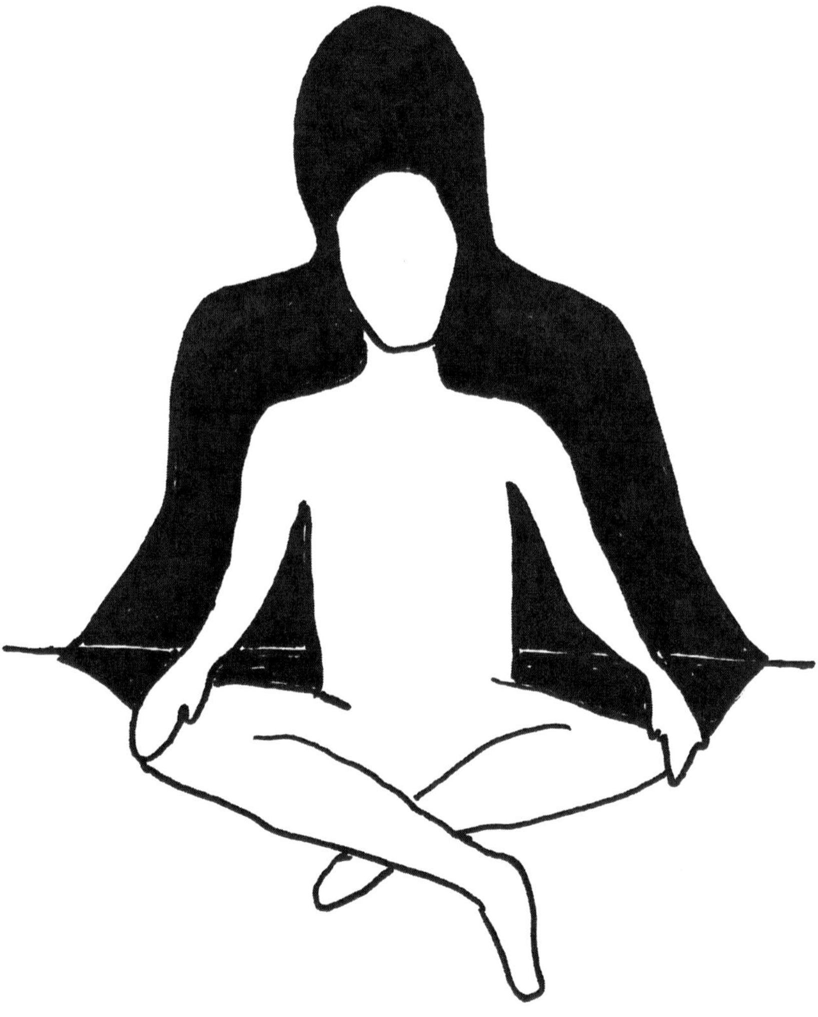

Fear

Fear is our own creation, something that doesn't exist in the external world. Basically, our fear is not about what is happening. Our fear is always about what's going to happen. It is fear of fear. That's why we can say that fear is something that is created by individuals and is private. If we investigate, we shall see that every person's fear is unique and individual. We don't accept any moment as it is now. Why we don't accept things as they appear to us has its roots deep in the first fundamental mistake made as human beings. From birth on, we make an "I" that is made from form, and we forget that we are divine consciousness. That imaginary "I" creation is man-made and incomplete. Because we cherish that "I," the need has been created to add things to that incomplete "I" in order to complete it or fix it.

Now we need a mind that is going to judge everything and everyone in order to see what is needed to be added. That's why we go to our judgmental mind all day long and all the time. We cannot accept any moment as it is unless it has the stamp of the judgmental mind. We don't know that when we accept the moment as it is. We allow the wisdom of life to work through us. When we judge, we stop the flow of the energy of life. By adding more objects of desire to that incomplete "I," not only does it not get complete, it creates more incompletion.

It's like we are thirsty and trying to quench our thirst with salty water. The moment that we start to talk, we are creating more incompletion. All our talk is about form in the external existence. What we believe from ourselves is only the picture of us. If we need to judge and create good and bad, let us do that wisely and send this message to our judgmental mind:

- Whatever is creating delusions, sorrows, or pain is bad. Whatever allows the flow of wisdom of life is good.
- Whatever has conflict with the physical and mental world is bad. Whatever allows us to accept things without any judgments is good.

We need to understand that any event happening at any given moment is connected to the physical and mental world. If we only focus on what is happening on the surface, the physical world, we are connected to the form consciousness. If we are connected to the space underneath all physical appearances, beyond the ideas of good and bad, that's the zone where we can transcend all the elements and events and be free from their influences. Getting connected to that zone, that's where we will see nothing but light and the sweetness of it.

Because we are operating on the physical level, we are attached to that form-made "I" and all of its possessions that we need to protect. One of our biggest fears is to lose any of the accumulation of this "I." We only add to this "I." Not only do we add possessions like properties and objects of attachment, but also status and titles. If we don't wake up from the dream of "having and doing" in order to get happy, if we don't wake up in our being now, someday we'll realize that we've been metamorphosed by the attachment of that imaginary "I."

Every object of attachment that we are adding to that "I" shall create more fear of losing one more thing. Our fear collection gets bigger the older that we get because of more accumulation of stuff, all because we have fallen into the trap of the "I" that is pretending to be us. Why in the world do we need competition if we didn't want to satisfy that "I"? If one of our children doesn't get attached to that "I," we start to teach them about it.

Children learn early in the family about competition because they observe how their parents are competing with relatives, neighbors, and each other. Every competition is adding to our fear collection. When we compete, there is a chance we'll lose, and the "I" doesn't want to lose. If we truly want to get rid of our fear, we need to get rid of competition and that "I" that needs to compete.

Because we created that "I" and we came away from our true self, divine consciousness, we lost our immortality and became the mortal "I." The biggest fear of all came with this creation: the fear of death. All our fears are traced back to that one fear, the fear of death. The roots of all our conscious or subconscious fear is the fear of death.

Let's say our biggest fear is the fear of losing our job. Sit for contemplation and go through all the possible misery that could come from that loss. You go through all the loss that comes from losing the job, such as bad credit and losing the car, the house, and all the possession. Okay, now you are homeless and on the street with no food and shelter. What fear is left now? Fear of sickness or suffering? Go through that as well.

What is left? At the end, it is always fear of death. When we are living in divine consciousness, we are immortal because death exists only in the physical world. The moment we created "I," we also created death.

Just remember one thing: there is no death. What we call death is nothing more than another constellation of existence. Many constellations happen in the physical plain, and they are matter-oriented. But what about the constellations and configurations that happen on the nonmatter level, on the level of unmanifested energy?

Fear patterns are woven in the energy level like a spider that makes a web, and that web becomes its universe. We get a fear thought, start to spin around it, and sit frozen in that web. Yes, fear freezes us. In the case of the spider web, the spider is not frozen. It's just waiting. As a matter of fact, the spider is very alert and alive. If some tiny insect enters the web, very quickly and with agility, the spider will move toward it and catch it.

In our case, we get frozen by the thought of the fear before the arrival of any incident in our reality, or web. We are dry drowning. Statistics show, in about 70 percent of cases of death by drowning in water (river, lake, or even swimming pools), victims have no water in their lungs. These dry-drowned victims' lungs were fully capable of delivering oxygen for staying alive. The real cause of their death had been fear of their death, not actual death.

Is this dry drowning the only case of premature death, or do we have more cases like these? What about many, many cases in India of people dying not from the venom of a snake, but only from the snakebite. If we look around us carefully, we'll notice that many people stop their dream job or dream trip because of the fear of failure, not because they failed.

Fear of failure makes us fail, and fear of death brings death to us. If we travel and listen to the people from different cultures, we'll notice that people with an old culture and history have more sayings and idioms about fear. The older the culture, the more people from that culture noticed the emptiness of fear.

One of the greatest idioms says, "Fear is the brother of death." It means that fear and death are each other's close companion. All these sayings from different cultures remind us that we should not exercise our fear. If a fear thought tries to merge into our mind, we shall drop that thought immediately and don't allow construction of any fear web.

If we take a fear thought and follow its scenario, like a spider spinning its web, we are constructing the fear web. The more scenarios we create, the stronger the web becomes. We should never forget that, when we are following or creating a fearful scenario, we are constructing a web that can only trap us.

We should not believe any thought that visits our mind, but rather every thought that visits our mind should believe in our being. That's why it's so important to sit quietly when we are peaceful and content and then contemplate to decide which thoughts have the right code to enter our minds (and which ones don't).

If we start to analyze every thought that might appear in our mind, then we will waste many precious moments of our life on thoughts that don't matter—thoughts that are not ours or don't give us anything. We shouldn't follow any thought unless we know that it is the kind that our peaceful and contented mind could have generated as well.

We need to find out which thoughts are worth following when we are content and not engaged in any thought process. We can develop a sensor in our mind that can discriminate between the thoughts. Many of us still don't have the understanding that being cautious or careful is totally different than being fearful. The quality of carefulness and alertness is totally different from the quality of fear. Right now you may be in that kind of situation, where you don't know if the current thought is one of care that you need to keep or is a wasteful thought of fear.

Of course, it is so hard to say for sure which one is which. That's why we all need to develop a thought indicator. The indicator, which knows the different thought qualities, can easily discriminate between the thoughts and identify which one is which.

Just imagine a brave crow that has developed so much courage that he can sit on the shoulder of the scarecrow and is brave enough to investigate the scarecrow's head with its beak, finding straw. Only this crow is entitled to triumph and victory, to celebrate the emptiness of fear. Other crows need to follow their own fear scenarios long enough until one day, just when the time is ripe, courage fills up their being and they investigate and recognize the truth.

Once the internal scarecrow has been dropped, the external scarecrows become empty as well.

Fear Meditation

Sit in a quiet place where you are warm and comfortable. In this meditation, we are focusing on our exhalations. We exhale deeply and freely with our eyes closed. We exhale only and allow the body to inhale for us. With every exhalation, we breathe out one of the elements of our fear. For example, if we are afraid to lose our house, then the object of our meditation is the house. With every exhalation, we let go of some of the belongings, things, or occupants of the house. We may start with furniture or carpets. At the last exhalation, we let go of the entire house, right down to the foundation. This meditation should be done at least a couple of times in order to be able to let go of the fear object completely.

The duration of the meditation could be about twenty-one minutes. You may think what about the fear of safety, the loss of independence, the fear of being robbed, or the loss of someone. Sure enough, your list may be even longer than this. Remember, it is not about how many faces and appearances that fear may have. It's about experience, and understanding that our fear is empty and an illusion. It's about experience that our fear, whatever kind it is, is vulnerable and breakable.

With the light of mindfulness, we can penetrate the fear and break it down. Truly all that we need to do in this powerful meditation is not to approach the fear in the usual way, to see it as unbreakable and impenetrable as a mighty whole and complete. With the light of wisdom, we break it into segments, fractions, and portions. Each and every fraction would sit in the center of our exhalations and would be sent back to the universe for recycling.

Even if the fear is the biggest scarecrow and cannot be approached in its entirety, we can divide him up by his hat, shawl, pipe, and shoes. It is all about understanding the truth, that *the whole is greater than the sum of its parts*. Practice this meditation to experience the freedom of letting go of the burden of the illusion of fear.

If we are facing a terminal illness and our mind is wrapped up with it so much that we need a more powerful meditation, something that needs to go even deeper than fear itself, we may use the following meditation. Throughout spiritual history, many masters and even enlightened beings have emphasized this meditation. The promise is not only to regain our freedom back from our fear, but also reach the state of detachment and enlightenment.

Lay down comfortably in a warm and cozy place. Let the arms recline alongside your body with the palms face up or the best as you can to imitate a dummy or a corpse. Find your breath. Catch your exhales, and exhale only. And let the body inhale for you.

After a while, when you have reached a state of peacefulness, let go of your self-grasping and observe yourself as a lifeless body, a corpse. Bring your attention to the toes, and observe the fire that has already started from the toes. The fire that is rising upward is burning the corpse to ashes. Ashes and fire are rising up from the corpse, and not even a trace of ash is left of the corpse.

Gradually the fire has reached midway and is still moving upward. Eventually we observe the whole process of burning the corpse to ashes and ashes to nothing. Nothing is left—no corpse, no ashes, and no fire. Stay in that state as long as you are guided to. Rise out of the meditation when it's time.

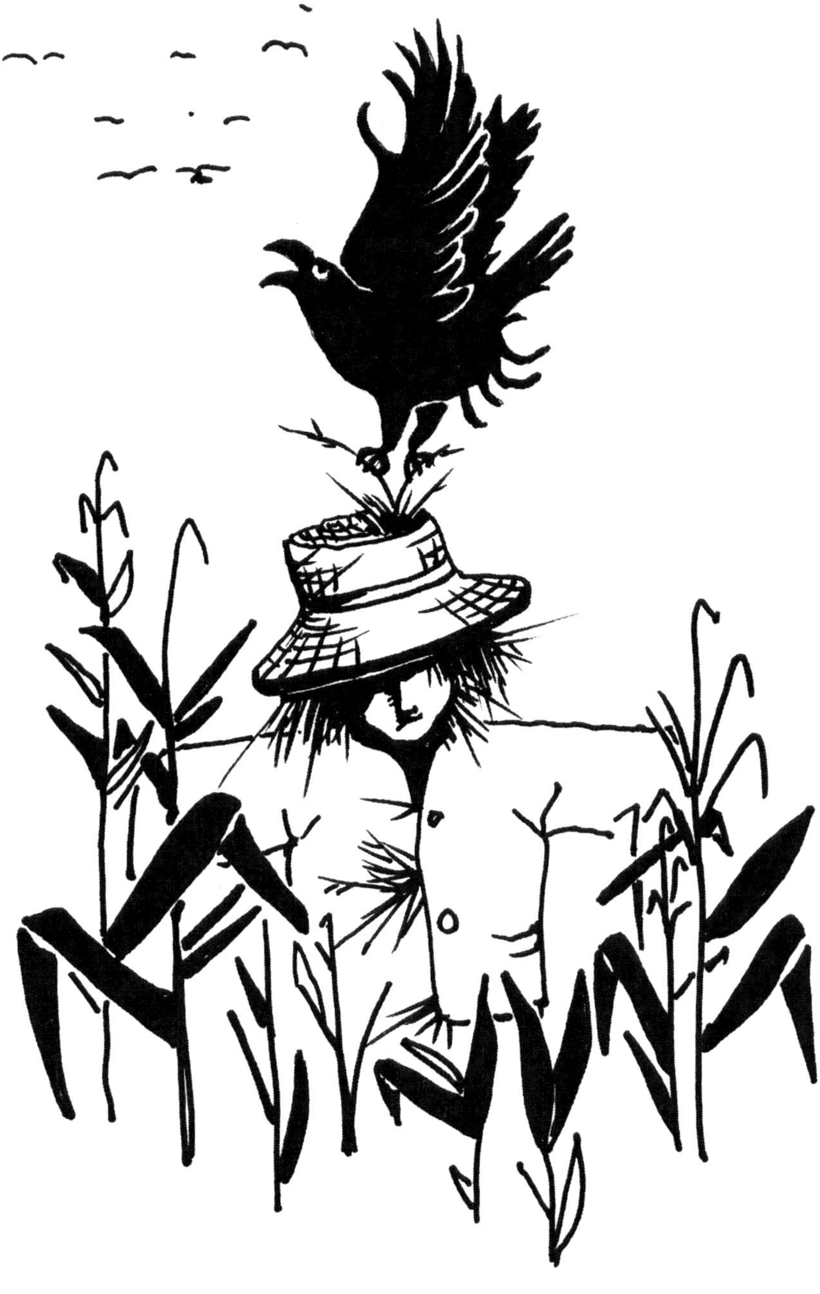

Remembering and Forgetting

Life is about forgetting and remembering. But what shall we forget, and what shall we remember?

A nurse is married and has a couple of children. When she goes to work, she forgets about the games or so-called duties of being a mom and wife and remembers her patients and what she's supposed to do at her job. When work is over, she comes home, and she forgets the hospital and patients. She remembers the family and being a mom to her children and a wife to her husband. She's not supposed to bring the hospital or the sick patient challenges into the bedroom or kitchen.

It so hard to believe that this is our first life. We have been many places, pleasant and unpleasant, and have done many things, both good and bad. Our life in the form that we have lived in has been taken away from us many times. We also have taken away many lives. So, do we want to remember everything? We had many, many pleasant moments that we have just forgotten. Life is about remembering and forgetting. We want to remember the lessons, the teachings of the wrong and immature things we have done, but we also want to forget our bad deeds.

This push and pull are necessary for a healthy and dynamic flow that is essential to a healthy and organic life. Sometimes there is no organic healthy life within this dynamic flow, but it's a grinding conflict.

For example, a friend has been trying to quit smoking for decades. What she does is that she wants to give up smoking (forgetting smoking), but what she really does is remember smoking because she smokes. She doesn't know one truth: "You cannot forget something by remembering it." For instance, a person may be watching a dramatic movie, and he or she is drawn in so deep that in one of the battlefield scenes a spark of a previous life emerges, one of being on a bloody battlefield.

Immediately this person takes himself or herself out of that zone, of remembering the battlefield and his or her vow to never go to war for any reason. This person forgets the war but remembers to never go to any war.

There are so many great moments from our previous lives that we may have forgotten because humans tend to cling to negative stories. There is no trace left of all the delicious ice cream in childhood. But the ice cream that we wanted to get, but didn't, is in front of our eyes as if it were this morning. All the toys that we played with are forgotten. We forget the teddy bear that we held in our arms as we fell asleep, but we remember the toy that we wanted, but didn't get.

We keep forgetting the lessons and teaching, and what we remember is the pain. We are missing the point. Every painful event that we've had, the ones that have ever happened to us, was there so we could fish out its lessons and remember the teaching. We forget the lessons and remember the pain again and again.

We need to empty in order to be able to fill up. A short story tells us about the professor from the West who went to a Zen teacher to learn about the Zen teaching. His intellectual mind was very active and present, but he had no meditative moments, like many people in the West. He couldn't even sit quietly for a couple of moments.

The Zen master felt the professor's bright intellectual mind, but he also felt his anxiety and restlessness. At the meeting in the Zen garden, the master offered some tea to the professor, and he started to fill up the cup. Once the cup was full, the master continued to pour more tea in the full cup. Eventually tea overflowed the lip of the cup and saucer and the table and was dripping on the professor's leg.

The professor started to yell at the Zen master, "Don't you see it's full? Why are you continuing to fill something that is already full? Don't you see the mess?"

The Zen master very peacefully replied, "That is you, my friend."

First you need to empty yourself from the daily activities, racing and competing that has been occupying your mind, and meditate. Go and empty your cup and then return.

We empty in order to fill.
We forget in order to remember.
We remember in order to forget.
We remember in order to remember.

Remember what you are remembering. If you are remembering something from the physical world or if you are recalling the creator and the creation, there are only two mantras: "Remember" and "Forget." Remember the creator in everything you see and think. Remember the angels, and forget the monsters. Remember to remember, and don't forget to forget.

When we are in nature observing a magnificent sunrise or sunset, the shimmering effect of afternoon light on the water, and the magical colors of the clouds in the sky, moments like these make us forget all our daily activities and remember the source. Deeply observe a puppy or a kitty jumping or playing with a toy or a piece of string, being fully and completely there with no thoughts. Being completely in their being brings us closer to the spirit so we may start to remember to remember and get connected to the Source. That's why we need to be in nature, so we stay natural.

What happens if we are sitting in the front of a computer for hours every day? Are we becoming more natural, more flexible, or more relaxed? Are we remembering what we are practicing to remember? Sometimes we should remember what we are doing and remember who we are. "Remembering and remember." Sometimes we need to stand up, so we can go through the slow range of motion of any kind and bring the Qi to every possible range of motion of our being. That's the secret of life.

Wherever you go, whatever you do, and whomever you see, remember to give a drop of your divine nectar to them. That's the key to bring divine light, wisdom, and mercy to everything and everyone.

There are two ways to remember, whether we are remembering the physical world, our stories, our activities, or a list of things to do that we are writing on a piece of paper or have written on our memory, part of our mind. That's all remembering the world.

The second type of remembering is to remember the Source.

Remember the creator or creation. Remember the spirit or the essence. We are currently so occupied with the world that we don't even realize that our time and resources as well as all our efforts and intelligence go toward remembering the world.

Remembering and Forgetting Meditation

Sit quietly in a quiet place where you will not be interrupted. Say to yourself,

> I am sitting here to forget all the strings attaching me to negative memories, thoughts, and emotions and to remember the divinity, the immortal spark inside. The purpose of my sitting here is to bring me into the present moment and to let go of things I need to forget. I'm also calling things to myself that I need to remember. I shall forgive and forget and let go of any people or events that are bringing me negative thoughts or emotions. I shall not give anyone any fear or any negative emotions of mine, not even a droplet in any plane of reality in the physical, emotional, or spiritual realms.

Sit long enough that you feel lighter and all negative-charged thoughts and emotions have left you before you go to the second part of this meditation. Also say to yourself, "I will remember only the goodness of people, especially my friends. I shall remember to radiate my positive vibration and give a drop of my joy and blessing to everyone I come across, physically or in my thoughts and mind."

Sit as long as you need before rising out of the meditation.

River of Life

Buddha always reminds us about the fleeting and impermanence of life. He says life is like a river; it flows and changes. Whoever doesn't accept the flow and changes will suffer more. Not only do changes happen in the seasons and nature, spring or winter, and the physical realm, they also occur in the emotional and mental plane.

Changes happen all the time and everywhere. Not only outside of us, but also inside and inside of the inside of us. The river of life flows and changes all the time and forever. Some of the changes are small and tiny and not noticeable, while some others are big and unbearable, so it can even change the structure of the substances and lead them toward transformation. At first glance, it looks scary when we notice that nothing is as solid and steady as we thought. Even the solid ground underneath our feet is a moving planet, moving through space and time.

Endless changes happen throughout our life, and there are more to come, unbearable events like the loss of family members and close friends. To think about these, we may become dull, passive, or even depressed. We may even think life is not fair, and it doesn't make any sense at all. Even those kinds of thoughts are yet another change in us.

Thoughts are changing us, and in the emotional scales, we move up or down. Thoughts are also changing us in the mental planes. The change of thoughts in any of these realms may cause transformations in the physical plane and physical body. For instance, the decision in your mind to faithfully attend yoga classes will manifest change in your physical body.

Basically, every bad or good, minor or major, or insignificant or groundbreaking thought changes us in a way that we may go down or up in our emotional or spiritual realities. Going down means we go lower in our self-esteem, getting more negative. Going up means to learn what we need to learn from that event and move forward and on—without carrying negative feelings, emotions, or any negative memories within us.

Sometimes we walk away from events, storing them up in our muscle memory. If the event impacted us deeply, the hook of that event sits in us in the form of bio-memory. The really groundbreaking catastrophic events may go even deeper and become our bio-energy. It is so important to live consciously so we can discern which event we allow to become part of our bio-memory. If something has gone so deep inside of us that it has entered our inner space, sure enough that phenomenon has the power and ability to accompany us from past to future.

Basically, we are having a memory-thought from the past and projecting that to the future. Unfortunately, almost all of our great, joyful events from the past have already passed, whether we carry some faint memory of them or no memory at all. Our tendency is to collect the unpleasant ones and weave them into a thought-memory blanket that can spread itself out and cover our future. If we allow this to happen, we are getting the default from the past and making that the future.

We forget that our current thinking makes up our reality. If at any given moment we notice that truth, we are floating on the eternal river of life, and our current thoughts make up our reality, we shall naturally attract:

- thoughts that hold more virtue and goodness for everything and everyone
- thoughts that are more vital to the environment and the planet, *and*
- thoughts that are messengers of survival for future life—not only for a few polar bears or a few remaining leopards—but give us certitude for the continuation of all kinds of life on our planet.

These thoughts carry the seeds of potential vitality. Now if we catch ourselves carrying a negative thought, we may remind our self that we are not exchanging wisely.

Misery is when we give a portion of our life as the present moment and receive a negative thought not only one single time, but recall that thought again and again.

One of the greatest masters of all time, Zoroaster, promised us that the key to enlightenment is within pure thought, pure speech, and pure action. This great master put these virtues in this order because, as we spoke of, first we pick up a thought to move through time and space. And if we pick up the same thought again and again, eventually it becomes our memory and bio-memory. We may have many thoughts, but not all of the thoughts come to the level of speech.

Speech is more subtle than thought. We may have many, many great thoughts for a public speech, but only small fractions of these thoughts can be delivered as a public speech. By the same token, we may have many great pieces of advice and hold a long speech about them. Yet when we are ready to follow the speech and take action, suddenly all of our wisdom may disappear before engaging in the action.

When some event from the bio-memory level fuses itself in the level of bio-energy, then naturally actions happen. When we accidentally touch a hot stove, it takes no time before the action of pulling the hand away follows it.

We never go through the slow-motion process to think, *Oh, I shall take away my hand*, deliver it to the level of speech, *Ahhhhhhhh!*, and then finally physically pull the hand away. No, we touch the stove and almost at the same time, without thinking, we pull the hand away.

When we practice our pure thoughts long enough, one day we will naturally evolve into pure speech, and sure enough, pure speech becomes pure action. These three virtues are not separate and independent from each other. They are, as a matter of truth, co-dependent, and sometimes one gives rise to the other. However, we always start with pure thought, but we need these three virtues to stay on the path of enlightenment and be able to walk our talk.

River of Life Meditation

Sit quietly in a relaxed position and contemplate, "My being is moving through space and time. The fuel of my being remains within my thoughts, speech, and actions. I'm sitting here to let go of any negativity that may have entered into my being and bring the purity and virtue back to my being."

Now start to focus on your breath. Find your breath, and breathe deep and freely. With every exhale, we breathe out our contaminations: any impure thought that we may have ever had, any impure speech we may have ever made, and any impure action we may have ever engaged in.

We ask the universe for forgiveness for any harm we have caused by our negative actions. (We don't want to fall into the hole of details.) Sit for this transcending meditation for as long as needed until the wish to become a disciple of the three virtues—pure thought, pure speech, and pure action—rises within you.

Sit as long as you need before rising out of the meditation.

Fact and Truth

To understand the difference between fact and truth, we need lots of contemplation and meditation to be able to look behind the veils. We need to tap into the wisdom behind the words because one may call "fact" superficial truth or even relative truth. It's not that much about words; it's all about looking behind the words to understand the dynamic of the operation. The way that we operate our life basically determines if we are attached to the facts or if we have embraced the truth.

Of course, facts are aspects of the truth, mostly an account of experience but not the totality. Once we experience the finality of existence, even the experience of finality fades away, and we merge into totality, the truth. But we need to be awake because, if we are sleepy, the facts will represent themselves as being the truth. Mostly human beings operate based on facts. We get a bunch of facts and declare them as being truth.

The way we operate in life is comparable to a fish. A fish is in the ocean but doesn't know it. It doesn't know that, not only are they swimming in water, they are living in the life-giving water. Now the fact is that the fish lives in water. That is an opportunity that the universe has granted to the fish, but it only becomes truth when the fish knows that it is living in water.

The *actual knowing* is the combination of the knower and the known. A fish that swims and sees water, "the known," is only part of the truth. The fish that not only sees water, "the known," but also knows itself, "the knower," is much closer to the truth. It's a fact that we are alive, but not truth.

We all have seen sleepwalkers, people who are not aware of others. They have no sensitivity at all for friends, family, or mankind. They are not aware of their own heart. They don't know they have a heart in their chest. Even their love is about what they will get in return. Their love is not true love, which is about giving and offering yourself unconditionally. No, their love is a business, a trade.

Even at the time, it looks like they are giving something. There is some calculating going on in their mind, how their actions will benefit them later on. Because a bunch of documents show these kinds of people are alive, the fact doesn't change the reality that is there is no aliveness in their actions, the truth. If we operate based on the facts, which is very common, we gather a bunch of facts about a person. Then we think we know that person.

We may think that, if someone gives us a bunch of facts about a particular object, therefore we know the truth about that object. But facts and truth do not always meet each other. As a matter of fact, most of the time, they don't. The truth goes beyond the appearances. The truth goes beyond appearing and disappearing. During the appearance of an optical illusion, something appears that is not true. What happens if, on a hot, sunny day, we get to see some water in a distance on the road, a so-called mirage? Naturally we continue to drive.

The experience has taught us "not everything that appears is the truth." There are also many things we don't see, but the truth is that they exist. For instance, we don't see love or compassion, but we feel their existence. We may see the great result of love and compassion, but the actual love or compassion are invisible.

Many people who have lost their parents report some kind of deeper connection that had first started after the so-called death, when the actual physical appearances disappeared. You, as the reader of this book, may belong to this group, experiencing your parents with a deeper connection.

It is a fact that our parents die, but it isn't the truth. Just because their physical bodies went through a transformation, that doesn't mean our true connections to them gets cut and disappears. Are they are gone with all their aliveness, activities, nonactivities, feelings, and emotions?

Fact vs. Truth Meditation

Sit in a comfortable position where you are not distracted with external circumstances and contemplate, "There are lots of facts that indicate I am alive. I am sitting here to go beyond all the facts indicating my aliveness and embrace the truth of my being."

First bring your attention to the physical body. Scan through it from head to toe, and transcend it. Then go through the emotional body. You will notice a shift in the physical body. The physical body responds by shifting the gears to deeper breathing or a sigh of relief "physically" or "mentally." Pass through the emotional body and move on to the mind. The third layer, the mind,[3] is much more challenging, but with sincere dedication and practice, you also will be able to pass through this layer too.

Sit long enough to go through the layers of physical body, emotional body, and the mind and receive a direct experience.

---

[3] To pass through the mind layer, we need to stop the thinking processes. (Don't worry. You will not die.) First you become alive when the state of having "thoughts" is changed to the domain of "being." Practicing to stop the thoughts is the biggest present you can give to yourself. Once you are trained enough in this, even during the day, you may take a break, stop moving, and stop the thought process for a brief moment. Then you can return to what you were doing. You will be amazed how much lighter and more focused you become.

One Plus One Equals One

This message will change your being and transform you. The first time you are presented with this, you may not understand it totally, but by opening this message and repeating it as a mantra, it will give you a key to a new dimension. The message is "one plus one equals one."

When we went to kindergarten, our teachers taught us "one plus one equals two," and at that moment, they created duality in us. We have been practicing that duality ever since. Everyone around us is believing and acting with the same concept and philosophy. Back through human history, we don't know when that duality started to add things together and create new things. Add one plus one, and create two out of that equation.

One may say, "Of course, one plus one equals two. Every shopkeeper, banker, office worker, and politician know that math."

That is the foundation of every society. When we go to big cities, we see construction everywhere. Everyone is building roads, shops, and houses, as if we didn't have enough and were in desperate need to have more. Why is that? Human history shows us, when nations get all the things they need, they start a war with the immediate neighbor nation or even nations far away. To have *more*, as if they didn't have enough. The moment we start to add one with one and create two out of that equation, we've created a new tool for our greed.

For example, I already have a house, but if I build another one or maybe three or four, it would be better. As a nation, we already have the land and all its resources, but if we colonize some other nations that have land with additional resources, mines that provide precious minerals, or reservoirs of oil, then we would be the richest and most powerful in the world.

Instead, if we knew that one house plus one house equals one house; one nation here plus one nation there equals one nation; or one culture plus one culture equals one culture, we would stop being greedy. We wouldn't have the need to add anything to ourselves in order for us to become complete. The need to add something to us came because of the separation that we made earlier, which created duality within us. We forgot that one plus one equals one, that it has always been one, and that it will always be one.

One may look at an apple tree and say, "There is much more than one apple on that tree."

If we look much deeper than counting the apples, we get to see there is one apple tree. We human beings decided to make many subdivisions to that tree and call them roots, trunks, branches, twigs, and fruit. If we look deeply within one apple, in the center of one apple, the apple tree is hiding itself in something that we call seeds. Truthfully, all apple trees are one. They all get nourished by a mother, which we call Mother Earth.

One may say, "But there is not only one planet in our solar system. We have many."

The truth is many, many drops gathered together to make one ocean. The drop is the ocean. The ocean is the drop. As above, so below. There is no end either way. Where is our solar system in the vast universe? Certainly, that is not the beginning or the end. It is the same if we open one apple and see the hidden apple tree in the center of it.

We may say, "The apple tree is the beginning, and this seed is the end."

We know that the apple tree was one day one of these that appears as a seed now. This cycle of tree and apple that we are observing is not the beginning or the end. It is somewhere in the endless cycle of appearing and disappearing.

Because of our limited knowledge about the unity and oneness of the universe, we have been dividing everything from everything else. We have even divided Mother Earth into many nations. We have even divided humanity into races and colors. Many nations mean many wars. Many races mean many conflicts. All the conflicts and wars in human history come from that fundamental mistake, not to see that we are all one.

Just imagine one day suddenly your body's right side says, "From today on, we are federal and separate from every other part of the body." Your right leg, right lung, liver, and right kidney—now the whole right side of the body—is separated from the rest. We would be lucky if the division is only right from left. Total chaos appears when every part claim independence. Right leg wants to go forward; left leg wants to go left. Right hand wants to grasp something, while left is dropping something. The heart decides not to provide nourishment to the lungs and right kidney.

Can you imagine that chaos? What happens when the body does not work as a unit? For instance, arthritis happens when the part of the body feels such a separation that it attacks and fights itself. The same happens if we forget we are all one nation with one mother and one home and go to war against each other.

Unfortunately, human history is full of that kind of insanity. There hasn't been only a first or a second world war. Actually, war never stops. The tactics change, but the war never stops. Remember the subdivision in the apple tree? Because of that fundamental mistake, the same subdivision comes to play on the earth. One nation on the earth is divided into many nations. The same subdivision for a single nation, south and north, is created—upper and lower class, female and male, black and white, and a lot more.

When does this subdividing end? Never. We can subdivide and separate one given thing forever. As above, so below. We need to practice to see things as complete and whole. Just enjoy things as they are. Appreciate them as they are. There's no need to change anything. Just embrace everything as it comes. When that happens, a deep sense of gratitude rises within us. We become thankful and grateful for everyone and everything around us. If the eye of our mind sees the oneness and completeness in everything, we drop the addictions of adding things to things in order to complete them. We come to the mind-set of one plus one is equal one.

One Plus One Meditation

One + One = One

This meditation can be done for one part of your body or the entire body. If you are doing this for the entire body, start from your forehead, going down through neck and shoulders; arms and hands; and then hips, legs, and feet. And then go to the internal organs, lung, heart, stomach, spleen, intestines, liver, and kidneys.

If you are doing this for only one part of the body, like your left foot or a sprained ankle, use the example below. Sit quietly in a comfortable position and contemplate, "I'm sitting here to let go of the duality and embrace the unity." Sit long enough that you are sincere about this statement.

Find your breath and quiet your mind. As you are breathing, notice how deep the breath goes, and send it even deeper. Notice that the breath is the fuel for your entire being. Allow your whole being and the breath to become one. Alternatively, send the breath to the left foot or the left ankle and the entire body while you are repeating this mantra, "One plus one equals one."

Continue the last step long enough that a sense of unity arises within you.

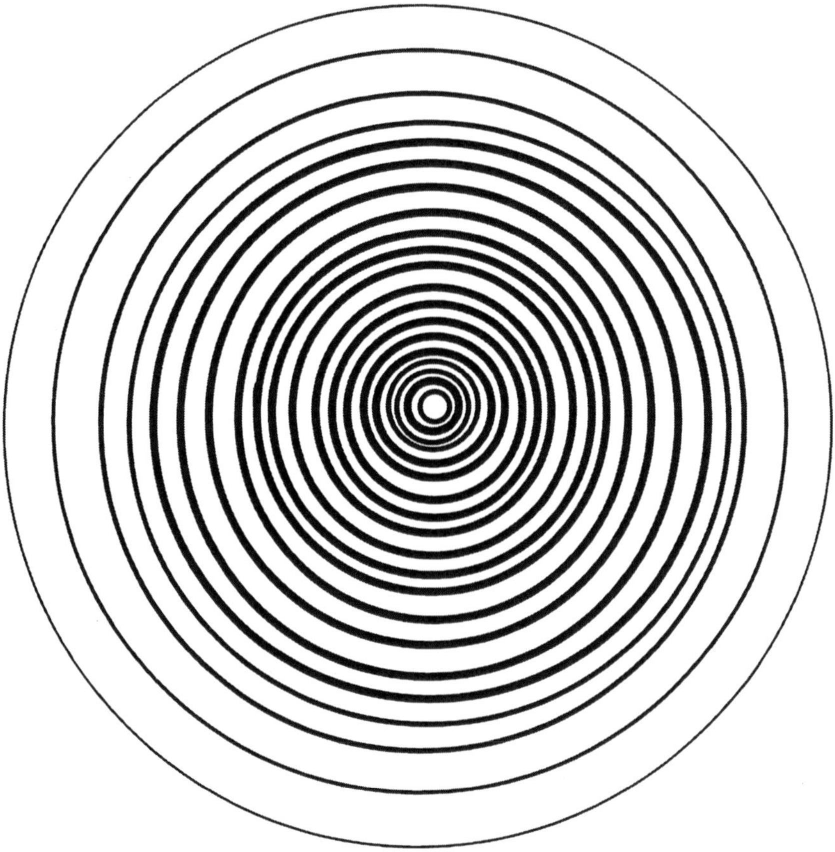

First Time

Everything that you see, do, and experience is for the first time. Just remember, the universe doesn't duplicate. In everything that is appearing, every event is unique, fresh, and alive. We human beings have copies and duplications. Even our names are someone else's name, as if we didn't have enough names in the archive of the universe. Even the weekday's names are duplications. When someone calls our name, we refer to the same image of our self. We never learn that there is such an abundance in the universe that the universe doesn't need to duplicate. There is such an affluence that even numbers that our intellectual minds have created get lost in it, and it becomes infinite. Numbers like Loshmitt's number, or 10^{26}, which is 1,000,000,000,000,000,000,000,000,000, get lost in the number of molecules and atoms of the air we are breathing in, in one single inhalation.

With such an abundance in the physical body, connected to our emotional body while putting the spiritual body on top of that, can you imagine what an infinite combination we are moving through? If we are the combination of body, mind, and spirit, we can imagine the abundance in our being. If we look at ourselves deeply, we shall find out that our beings offer themselves through the universe in an infinite range of being. This range of being (ROB) is the combination of our reality at any given moment and space/time awareness. Just imagine the combination of the physical body, emotional body, intellectual body, sexual body, and spiritual body, which are all different and unique, combined with space/time, which is always unique, making up our infinite ROB.

We approach every event as being mundane and casual—not unique, fresh, and vital—and for the first time. We do this for a couple of reasons:

1. Our ego is taking charge of every situation, even before we realize it. The ego claims to know everything. The all-knowing ego doesn't want to go through the humbleness of being the student and admitting there is a lot to take in. And there is a lot to learn and much to practice. No, the ego is already above everything else and knows how to deal with and handle every situation. Furthermore, ego has the quality of possession and ownership. Through the eyes of ego, everything that we are confronting belongs to ego. Not only does the ego own the people, but it also owns scenery, events, and even stories. Let's say a friend told us about the magnificent sunset at the horizon of the ocean with a beautiful blue sky. By delivering this story to someone else, suddenly our ego kicks in. The ego now owns the story—the sunset, the clear blue sky, and even the horizon. We would tell the story in a way as if everything were created by us. We may start telling the story with, "*My* friend told *me* ..." We haven't even started the story, and it already has two stamps of ownership attached to it. Because of that delusion of ownership, the aspect of our being that needs to embrace and welcome the first-time experience gets lost. That sense of being excited when we experience life for the first-time is now falling into the trap of grasping and the repeated story of ownership. That trap can vary in size from the highest caliber to the lowest, depending on where we are on the journey with the ego. The stronger the ego-based quality of the mind, the more reduced is our experience of the *alive*, the first-time experience.
2. We cannot arrive at the space/time awareness in order to go through the first-time experience because we are always conditioned with stories, and our connecting could be the attachment to or the hangover from our past stories or our projection of future stories. The physical appearance alone is not enough

to claim that we are truly present. The physical body without mindfulness is only the shell. Mental clarity and contentment are needed to be able to let go of our stories and see what the universe is offering us. Unfortunately, it's not only ego from one side and stories from the other side. Most of the time, these two merge into each other, and their combinations make a complex mixture of past stories/future projections/ego.

With this heavy combination, we could never taste the nectar of the first-time experience because we already have more on our plate than we can handle. There is no space for new arrivals. The present moment offers itself to us with all its goodies and adventures, but we are full and occupied. How is it now possible that we arrive and embrace the new vastness of it? First, we need to empty ourselves from occupation. Remember the chapter, "Remembering and Forgetting."

> We empty in order to fill.
> We forget in order to remember.
> We remember in order to forget.
> We remember in order to remember.

We need to forget our attachments and projections, and we need to remember that this moment is new, actually *brand new*. The universe offers itself in abundance and moves into infinity, unlike our limited ego. The tricky ego doesn't represent itself to us as being stingy, possessive, and controlling. It will represent itself as nurturing and careful of our safety, so we fall into its trap.

Zen Buddhism has lots of great stories and metaphors to clear out the cluttered mind. One of the greatest stories that really helps us to understand the potential of every moment is the following.

In a Zen monastery, the frustrated disciple came to the master, saying, "I have been in this monastery since my childhood. I have done everything that you've asked me to do, getting up at dawn, chanting, going to classes and practice during the day, and doing long meditations at night. Where is the enlightenment that you promised me? It looks like I cannot reach it alone or it's a fake promise. Either way, as you always tell us, whenever you catch the fish, it's fresh. I am fully ready to catch enlightenment. Either you give it to me now or I'm out of here. The bag with my few belongings is packed and waiting for me in the yard of the monastery."

Now the master, with a deep compassionate understanding, replied to the disciple, "As you know, enlightenment is nothing I can give to you, but I can offer you a way to reach it right now. But the question that remains is: are you ready?"

The disciple answered, "Of course I'm ready!"

The master said, "Not only listen to what I offer you, but do it. Do it with all your being. Go and drink a glass of water."

The disciple, totally frustrated and at the end of his rope, replied, "I knew that you would say something like that; therefore, I'm out of here."

In the yard of the monastery, the faithful and frustrated disciple looked around the Zen garden, reviewed all the long years he had spent in the monastery, and thought to himself, *I have done everything that my master has ever told me. Why did he tell me to drink a glass of water prior to my departure? I'd better drink this glass of water, fully and truly.*

Now with a glass of water in his hand, he asked himself, *could it be that all these years of training was to reach this moment, where the state of the mind that resides in the present moment is ready to give birth to the infinite? For my last act, I devote myself to do what the master has asked me to do.* "Get present, let go of the stories, and have no attachment or any hangover to the story. And when all of you has arrived completely, mindfully allow the drinking to happen by itself. Just be a true companion with the action of drinking."

Listening to this guidance, the disciple held the glass of water and was fully determined to do his last action in the monastery faithfully and mindfully, by allowing to receive fully and completely the first drop of water. Suddenly he experienced that this was his first drop of water in his life and not the last. All other glasses of water prior to this one had been only the act of consuming water.

It arrived around an empty shell. He realized that all his eating, drinking, sleeping, and actions in between had been shallow and had no anchors or roots in his inner space. He realized that the enlightenment had always been within and around him, in every flower in the

Zen garden, while he had been looking at them and dreaming about enlightenment.

Everything we are doing right now, it's for the first time, even if it looks like we have done it many times in the past. The same movement or action is only one of the factors for duplication. What about the many other factors that are combined with the action? Factors like place, time, temperature, and … We may be able to duplicate one or two factors of the whole, if any at all, but we could never duplicate the same original event or object twice.

Basically, we can never step into the same river twice. In the case of a river, it's easy to understand that, because the movement and flow of that river is so obvious, the hangover of the river may fool us again. Hangovers are things such as labels, names, or pictures. Human beings have names for everything. Everything has a name for us. Not only people, but also streets, houses, and rivers.

For example, if we have visited a river, that river gets stored into our memory with a name. Whenever we remember that river's name, we think we are recalling that same river. We forget that the river that we have visited has moved on right after we stepped in it. By the same token, if we are performing some action, that action is described as "doing something."

For example, every evening when we are watering the flowers, we may think we are doing the same thing. We forget that the only thing that is the same is the name, "watering the flowers." Even if it looks like it's the same because of the timing and the fact we are using the same watering can, the water is new and different. The flowers are different; our state of mind is different. Somedays we may not enjoy watering the flowers that much because we may feel obligated to be somewhere else or doing something that might be more important.

A curious Zen disciple in one of the monasteries thought, *our master always taught us that the universe doesn't duplicate. I wonder if each morning, at the same time I sit at the same place and draw the same flower woven in a tapestry, how long would it take to be able to duplicate.*

After twenty and some years, he had to give up that experiment because he realized that he may sit at the same place at the same time but had no influence over the weather, the reflection of the sun in the monastery, which disciple may enter the Gampa, if the birds were singing in the garden, or many other things that varied every time. Even his emotional state and mind-set was different; therefore, he could not deliver any duplication.

Meditation for the First-Time Experience

Sit quietly in a comfortable place where you can be for a while without any distraction or disturbance, like ringing phones or any alarms, and contemplate, "Every moment is different because my being in space/time is different. I lose the first-time experience because my ego is taking charge of every situation. I lose the first-time experience because I am always conditioned with my own stories."

After we've contemplated long enough and arrived at a meditative state, single-mindedly we want to meditate on, "Everything that arises in the vital present moment is fresh and unique with no repetition of any kind. I shall always remember these truths and know everything I experience, eat, drink, and attend is for the first time."

Searching vs. Seeking

We all have latent and blatant ideas about what searching and seeking is. But we should understand that these two terms are totally different. One is used in the worldly manner and conversation; the other is a term that is used in the spiritual quest.

Let's say we have lost our car key in the living room. What do we do when we begin a search? First of all, we make sure that there is enough light to see. If not, we turn on the light. If we find the key, does this mean that we are saved from ever losing our key again? Of course not. We may lose our found object again.

With the act of seeking, we also need light. But we turn on our *wisdom* light to shine on our seeking path. Once we experience what we are seeking for, we never lose it. We may search for many things, but they all have something in common. They are worldly. Soon they will be found, or we give up looking for them any longer.

When we are searching, we might get serious, but there is no seriousness with seeking. We might be passionate or sincere, but no seriousness to make seeking humorless or heavy. There are lots of examples of all kinds of seekers in many traditions. We've all heard many great stories of vision quests in shamanic traditions or the different tribes in native Indians.

Seeking doesn't have any particular religion or tradition. There have been seekers throughout human history and within mystical traditions. Now the question that comes with this knowledge is: what is the commonality between all the religions and traditions? They all recognize the transformational power of seeking, which sometimes goes even further than our foundation.

Seekers are the mystics within a religion. They are a bridge, connecting all the religions and traditions. Seekers by their seeking have an experience that is a drop and the ocean at the same time. There is a truth beyond every religion: the longing of the seekers is behind that truth. It all starts with a question: Who am I? What is God? Or is there life after death?

Having profound questions like these begin to deepen our knowledge and understanding. Because of the nature of these kinds of questions, we have to dive deep. Ecstasy and revelation are found in depth. Like the ocean, from the surface, we cannot see that much. The sunken treasure hunters know this truth. They know, the deeper they dive, the more precious the pearl.

When a profound question like "Who am I?" appears, we need to go through many layers of thoughts, emotions, and memories and seek through the foundation of our existence.

The first thing that happens with that question is that we begin to search for the physical "I." For example, for a seeker whose name is John, the answer would be, "You are John. You are thirty years old, the employee of a company."

That's all happening because we are searching and not seeking. That's why we fall into the story of our self. If an answer like this comes, we need to ask the same question again, "Who am I?" Now a different answer will appear, like, "You are a father or the son of ..." That is another story about us and not who we really are.

We ask the same question again, "Who am I?" Again, an answer comes. "You are a human being asking this question."

Eventually all the answers that come are based on thoughts, emotions, and memories. That's why many great masters encourage their disciples to ask the question "*What* am I?" instead of "Who am I?" If we ask "Who am I?" we already have assumed a lot about ourselves, like we are already a person.

But with the question "What am I?" we already have shed our ignorance that gives us the idea of separation from the whole. By nurturing the fire of seeking and coninuting to blow into that fire with a question like this, we open our self to a new dimension of reality, and the sacred secret unfolds itself into its infinite aspect of manifested and unmanifested energy.

This unfolding of sacred knowledge within us is what the seekers are behind. Our physical bodies have a beginning and an end, like everything else that we know. Our delusions such as anger, jealousy, and ignorance have no beginning. We don't know the beginning of our delusions or our illusions. We can only bring an end to them. Seeking is a vastness that has only a beginning and no end.

The Great Spirit, or divinity, has no beginning and no end. That's why the universe keeps expanding. Once the never-ending fire of seeking starts in us, we are transformed into a seeker who enjoys the ride of abundance, the ride of bliss. The seeker's internal reference point is not the ego (self-image) any longer; it is the pure consciousness of the Self.

The Self is the same spirit that has different appearances, faces, and disguises. With the question "What am I?" we get to experience this imperishable pure consciousness that is omnipresent in every step of our seeking. We blow into the fire of seeking every time we withdraw from daily life and look into our self with the same seeker's question, "What am I?"

When we sit back and look into our life, which direction are we headed toward? The power of seeking brings us to the conclusion, to change the direction if necessary. We may have a job for a long time or an established business that has brought us financial independence and allows us to go through life for a long time, but the job hasn't offered us the freedom that we have been longing for.

You, as a reader of this book, may belong to one of these people. Emotional freedom and creative freedom are essential fuels for a seeker. Here we must use our wisdom to differentiate between our boredom and seeking. The negative energy of impatience and boredom shouldn't fool us and represent itself as powerful energy of seeking. In today's world, people are changing their directions all the time. But it's not because of the power of seeking; it's because of unsettled energy of confusion and boredom.

If an awareness for changing direction comes from the power of *seeking*, that's a bliss. It doesn't matter how long and how far we have been cruising in the wrong direction. We need to stop, contemplate, and look for the right path for us. We should consider if the change would nurture the seed of divinity inside of us. If that is the message, then so be it. Do it with the power of your seeking.

Searching vs. Seeking Meditation

Sit quietly in a comfortable place where you can be for a while without any distraction or disturbance like a ringing phone or alarms, and contemplate,

- I understand that there is a truth behind every religion, and whoever wants to experience that truth has to let go of the stories about himself or herself and his or her religion. That truth remains in the foundation of every being.
- I have been missing that truth because I have been searching in the external world. I am sitting here to let go of all stories about the truth and allow the sacred knowledge within my being to unfold so I may experience the truth.

Now hold your focus on one of the above bullets that resonates with you the most and meditate on it. Sit long enough in meditation until you experience the freedom and vastness of the infinite.

Tree of Life

We all have seen a painting or a tapestry with a tree of life with different animals representing various beings and lifestyles. Just imagine if we expose a few people to an actual tree. They would all see that tree from their perspective. According to their reality, they would see what they want to see.

- A businessman would open a window to the potential profit and begin to evaluate the amount of fruit on the tree, followed up with thoughts like, *If I pick up the fruit and box them, they could be sold at market. What is the easiest and shortest distance for transportation?*
- A playful person or an athlete would climb the tree and have fun. An artist would get the artistic vibrations, and either he or she would begin to play music or sit under the branches and recite poetry.
- A painter would capture the beauty of the tree and start to paint the tree in its surroundings.
- A lumberman would think, *how big is the trunk? Is it big enough to get a sufficient amount of wood from? If I cut the tree, which direction will the tree fall?*
- A philosopher would ask himself or herself, *does this tree exist in the external world? Does it inherently exist?* Then he or she would start to debate about the existence and nonexistence of the tree.
- A biologist or forester would try to identify the species and categorize the leaves, shape, and so on.

- In the case of a person of authority, like a police officer, his or her operation would be very different. First the officer would look for unusual evidence, making sure that no one could hide himself or herself in the branches or behind the trunk. What could that orange-reddish spot be? A blood stain?
- A true meditator would see and feel the beauty and presence of the tree, enjoy the birds on the branches, and have respect for the hands stretched toward Father Sky and praise the existence. He or she would feel the roots that have merged into the body of Mother Earth, rooted and grounded within her body, and capture and transmit her vibrations. The person would let the tree know that its being and its beauty were appreciated and admired. If the meditator needed some grounding vibrations, he or she would ask the tree to give some of its accessible energy. Once permission had been granted, the individual would hug the tree and meditate, filling up his or her tank with the life-grounding energy.

These examples are not the only possibilities to approach a tree. If there are so many perspectives to view a tree, then we can imagine how many different ways we may open ourselves to life and view the tree of life. Our reality is such a dreamlike state. Many times we comprehend that something is not quite right in our view of life or our lifestyle.

Instead of looking deep inside of us and changing our perspective, we change the location. We move from one house to another or from one town to another. Or we change our objects of attachments. We change our car, furniture, or wardrobe, or we remodel a room or paint walls. We change our dreams.

We don't need to change our dreams. We only need to wake up. While we are dreaming, we don't know that we are just dreaming because it looks so real. We go to many beautiful places, meet different people, and visit the highest mountains, all while we are laying down on the couch. Although the physical body seems to have gone everywhere and done many things, we didn't move one inch.

How can we become aware that we are dreaming and that it is just another dream? If we have ever been on the stage playing a minor role, like at school or any other kind of performance, when you are on the stage, you know you are acting.

From the audience point of view, they are the observer, and you are the observed. From your point of view, you are the observer, and the audience is the observed. All the great actors try to get rid of the image of being the observed and only be the observer so they can create a fluid play. Amateur actors battle between the observer and being observed.

First, when the ego is on the stage of our mind, we are the observed, and the ego is the observer. If we merge into our ego, then the observer and the observed are one. Imagine sitting in our house and two thought-suggestions come knocking at our mind's door. One thought suggests to go outside and retaliate against our neighbor who was unfair to us. The second thought suggests to move on and forgive the neighbor.

Let's say we invite the first thought in and merge into that thought. Then we make it into a dough and bake it on the fire of retaliation. Finally, we munch on that poisonous bread until we are full of hatred and retaliation. Now we are outside the house and fighting the neighbor.

At that point, there is no separation between our ego and our self. We are the ego; the ego is us. The observer and observed are one. Before merging into any thought, just before entering into any dream or dreamlike state, when our cognition has not chosen any direction, we need to use the compass of our wisdom to see which direction we are going.

We have two internal reference points, or reference sources, at any given time: self and the Self. The lowercase self is based on our survival, worldly objects, and possession. It is ego-oriented. The uppercase Self is based on love, compassion, and wisdom and is divine or Spirit-orientated. We choose self over the Self most of the time. We get reminded by friends or family and pushed by the spouse and society. We get hijacked and bombarded by the media to choose self over the Self.

Now if the mind brings a thought and we don't engage with that thought, it's like the actor on the stage and we are the audience. If we don't engage with that thought, the mind will change the scenery and start to bring reasons or perform new acts so long that we finally get involved in that current thought. However, if we remain the determined audience and don't put any emotion, attention, or judgment on this, the mind eventually gives up.

But this is not easy because the mind knows not only all the cool acts perfectly, but also our weak points. The mind knows exactly what to say and do so that, without knowing, like in the case of sleepwalking, we take over the role that the mind has started. The good news is that there is a place where the mind cannot enter. The mind has never seen that place, even when we go there and come back. The mind doesn't notice where we have been. Every time we visit that place, we drop some of our delusions and illusions and come back much stronger. Every time we go there and come back, the mind gets surprised because it has to work harder on us. By going to that place again and again, we go beyond the notion of the observer and being observed. That place is meditation.

Meditation for Tree of Life

Sit in a comfortable place where you can be for a while without any distraction. Find a comfortable position, and contemplate,

- I'm sitting here to transcend all of my perspectives that are based on myself and worldly possessions and are ego-oriented.
- I'm sitting here to open myself to the highest cosmic energy, the Self, the pure consciousness. By changing the switch of my being, my reference point shall not be myself any longer, but instead the Self. Every thought, speech, or action of this being shall be according to that frequency and vibration.

Now hold your focus on one of the above points until you arrive in a meditative state and meditate. Sit so long in this meditation until you feel or enter the higher state of consciousness and vibrations.

Inner Space

When we hear *inner space*, we may think, *I cannot remember where that place was. Maybe I didn't pay attention in biology or anatomy class. Let me grab the human anatomy book and do research.*

We cannot find that place in any book. We need to study the spiritual anatomy in order to recognize that place. Because our nature and design is based on duality, we operate in two ways based on matter and the physical world, or Divine and Spirit. Our worldly personality has a name, an age, a Social Security number, and a job, and everything is based on the world, its possessions, and objects. All the activities—such as sports, shopping, working, and so on—are based on worldly possessions, objects, name, and fame. Everything in this world gets evaluated and classified. They are analyzed, numerated, and labeled. Everything is numerated in order to find its ranking, or its position, for its comparison. Everything falls into the category of good or bad.

The second operation is based on the spiritual values and is not worldly. That realm is possession-less and timeless and has no numbers. In other words, it is inclusive of all numbers. It's like the position of zero in mathematics. All the numbers come from zero. On one side of zero, the numbers, so-called "positive numbers," go up. And on the other side of zero, the numbers, or "negative numbers," go down. Zero is nothing, and yet it is everything. Zero is the balance and counterbalance for all numbers.

We go to two places based on our operation. One is our inner space; the other is our inner court. What happens when we go to our inner court? Just as with the external legal court, we experience lots of anxiety, struggle, and turbulence. The more frustrated and angry we are, the better it is for the inner court. The louder, the more unsettled, and confused we are prior to our arrival, the more welcome we are to the court audience and the judge.

Unlike the inner court, there is a requirement before entering inner space, and that is silence. If we are frustrated or angry, there is no chance of entering that domain. That's why many people hardly ever get the chance to visit that dimension. If we are serious about introducing ourselves to this magical place, we need to practice silence. We don't need to go to a silent retreat to practice silence.

We can practice at home. Do the short silence meditation every day, and on every other occasion, practice the longer meditation until you get your visa to enter that pure land. Unlike the inner court, which is all about having or doing, the inner space is all about being. By visiting inner space, our being gets rejuvenated, refreshed, and expanded. There is no judge in this space. We may get reminded or be gently guided, or maybe the light of wisdom shines on some areas to bring us clarity, but there would be no judge or judgment there. The infinite clarity doesn't need any judgment.

We may choose one path out of only two possibilities, which in itself may bring us to the judgment that we have chosen the right path and the other path would have been misleading. Or we chose one path out of thousands. Then we have more tolerance because just a few of the other options not chosen would have been okay. Our tolerance will increase, and the judgmental mind will fade away and become less colorful with the more choices we have.

The fewer the possibilities, the louder the judgmental mind. Because inner space expands itself over all the infinite dimensions and all the infinite possibilities, therefore there would not be judgment there. Because we go for refuge to one of these two places, the inner court or inner space, consciously and subconsciously, we nurture them too. All we need to do is to observe our diet, especially our mental diet. As an example of observing our diet is the Cherokee legend of "The Wolf Within."

Once a Cherokee grandfather revealed the challenging human battle with all its ups and downs to his grandson this way.

"There is this ongoing fight inside of me between two wolves. One wolf is ego-centered and evil and has qualities such as hate, anger, jealousy, greed, arrogance, superiority, self-pity, and fear. The other wolf is not ego-centered and has peaceful qualities such as love, compassion, generosity, kindness, humility, serenity, hope, and faith. The longer I live, the more battles I experience."

The grandson was very concerned and asked the grandfather, "But tell me, which wolf will win?"

The wise old man answered, "The one that I feed. And remember, the same fight goes on inside every human being, including you."

Every day we engage in many activities, we go to work, socialize, go places, watch TV, and listen to music. Before, during, and after any activity, we can ask ourselves, "Which wolf am I feeding? Am I feeding my inner space or my inner court?"

Let's say we watched a horror movie and forgot to ask that question at the beginning or during the film, but we still have the chance to ask that question after the movie is finished. Close your eyes and let your mind wander. Just watch your mind and where it goes: to your inner court or your inner space.

By the same token, we look at all our other activities to find out which wolf we are feeding. By observing closely our external activities, we can recognize which inner domain is dominant. It's a two-sided street. Inner space is nourishing outer space; outer space is nourishing the inner space. Inner court activities guide us to external court and all the turbulence and chaos in our external world. The struggle and violence in the external world feeds our inner court.

How can we break this cycle? What is the medicine here? The eighth-century Buddhist monk, Shantideva, gives us the following medicine. He says, "When you are walking on the seashore and the shells and rocks are hurting and injuring your feet, you have two choices: whether you can cover the entire seashore with leather and protect your feet or put leather on the soles of your feet, allowing you to walk everywhere without being hurt."

Similarly, we are unable to control the external world. All we need is to be at ease and peace in our inner world. What need is there to restrain anything else?

First of all, we need to understand the cycle and see that we are the combination of inner and outer world. And then we contemplate and meditate to make a strong wish to come out of the negative cycle. By putting our willpower behind the wish, now we can engage in practicing silence and watching our diet (physical and mental). Because of the power of habit, it's not easy to stop our activities right away or to kiss it goodbye forever.

For example, if we watch TV every night, to break that habit and replace it with a healthier habit would be challenging. That's why we need to practice silence and meditation. But remember, by putting our willpower behind the wish, victory is ours. Breaking the cycle should start from inside; therefore, we need to practice with our inner space first.

After getting familiar with that wonderland inside, naturally we are drawn to listen to the raindrops falling on the roof rather than listening to the evening news. We are naturally drawn to the silence of our garden rather than the noise in a movie theater. Again, breaking through the negative cycle should begin from inside. One of the waves, or ripples, generated in our inner space is enough to change all of the external unhealthy habits.

Inner Space Meditation

Sit quietly in a comfortable position where you are not disturbed by anyone, you have no interruptions from the phone, and you are comfortable and will not need to change your position for a while. Then contemplate,

- I know by going to my inner court where I become judgmental, angry, anxious, and stressed. I know that the judge and inner court exist because I feed them. Every time I visit the inner court, I have given my stamp of approval to its existence.
- Every time when I connect with the inner space, I become peaceful, and my horizon expands. Visiting the inner space reminds me about my being, being connected to all dimensions, and becoming timeless with no label. Inner space offers me freedom.

Contemplate the above statements long enough until the wish of entering inner space will rise within you. Now the actual meditation begins when you are single-mindedly focused upon that wish. You are focusing on that wish without falling into the details. As soon as you realize that the mind has taken you away from the meditation object, the wish, you bring your focus back to the wish.

Again and again, the mind may trick you, but with the mindfulness, you bring yourself back to that wish. Meditate long enough until you recognize that the foundation has been created within you. Rise out of the meditation but water that *wish plant* during the day whenever you remember. and again and again through practice the same meditation again and again.

Gratitude

What is gratitude? If someone does a favor for us and we thank that person, are we showing gratitude? Gratitude is much deeper than just being polite or even thankful. It goes much deeper than the social etiquette, the familiar status, or the articulation of our thanks in a nice, kind, soft voice. It goes much deeper than showing affection for a game of business of give-and-take. It's not about getting a gift on Christmas and now we are thankful, therefore we are in a state of gratitude.

There are lots of stories and metaphors in Sufism about gratitude because the center and focus of Sufism *is* gratitude. One of the great stories is about a Sufi master and his three disciples who went for a spiritual wandering. Traditionally when a disciple or a dervish goes for a wandering, he takes a vow to not take any food or possessions with him. He goes with the faith that the universe will provide, and because the community is aware of his vow, compassionate people offer him food, drink, and shelter for a short time or, on occasion, the night.

The Sufi master and the disciples took their vow and went on their spiritual wandering. At the end of the first day, without food or shelter, they crashed somewhere in an open field. Before sunrise, the disciples woke up, wondering why their master was giving thanks to God.

They whispered, "Maybe he's giving thanks for the food in advance for the new day."

The second day brought neither food nor shelter. And again, the disciples rose before the sunrise to the sound of their master praying. Now the disciples were suspicious about their master and thought maybe secretly he had gotten access to some food that they didn't know about.

On the third day, not only did they not get any food or a place to rest, they were also were insulted by people and accused of being a community parasite and useless beggars.

Exhausted and at the end of their ropes, they crashed in a cemetery near a village from where they had been kicked out. The next day, before sunrise, the half-dead disciples were wakened by the prayers of their master, crying and praising God.

The frustrated disciples came to their master, saying, "You may think you are fooling yourself, us, or God, but we have watched you for three days, and we know you didn't get anything to eat either. But now we are close to death, and we don't understand your thanks. Is it for the food that we didn't get, or is it for the insults and name-calling by the villagers?"

After listening compassionately to the hungry disciples, the master replied, "I am not expressing my gratitude for these three days. My gratitude is for before these days. I came empty-handed to this world. The universe has been taking care of me so generously. It didn't gift me with only hands, feet, and eyes alone, but also granted me a heart through which I can communicate directly to the universe. The universe has been taking care of me the whole time because, like all the other babies born, I wouldn't have been able to drink, eat, or grow up by myself without the kindness of others. It is impossible to give thanks to the midwife, the people who took care of me when I was little, and all the helpers and teachers on the path. Of course, I didn't go through all the details, but still I haven't reached the point where I've gotten to express my gratitude for these three days that the universe has put us on the waiting list.

"By the way, this state of gratitude that I'm expressing is not for what I do or don't have or what I do or don't do. It's not for any gain or loss. This is the deep overwhelming feeling inside of me, overflowing and connecting with the existence. It is the individual expression of *being*. Just *being* by itself alone is enough reason to be grateful."

If we read this story again and again, as if it is the water and nourishment for our internal gratitude-seed, eventually it starts to flower inside of us. If we listen carefully, this master is handing us our ticket to freedom, the ticket that allows us to enter our being and leave the hustle and bustle of "having and doing" behind.

He says, "This deep gratitude that I'm expressing is not for any gain or loss. It's not for what I have or don't have or what I do or don't do. It is my individual expression and response to my very being."

Here he points out the universal truth of the three anchors of existence: doing, having, and being. If we go to nature and sit beneath a tree and then drop all our activities, finished and unfinished businesses, and thoughts and ideas of our possessions (what we have or don't have) and go for refuge to our *being*, suddenly we start to connect with the other beings. We would not only feel the tree, the field, the insects, and the birds, but also the white clouds drifting in the sky.

They would feel so close that we'd think we could reach them with our bare hands. That state of being is complete, and it doesn't need anything to be added or removed. It's the complete circle. The state of being is enough to make us content and blissful. The access to that state gets easier if we go to nature or a retreat, but not necessarily do we need to go anywhere or do anything. We can *be* wherever we are right now. We don't need to go to a monastery or be a monk or holy being to reach that state. All we need to do is unshift the gear of "having or doing" and experience our natural state, the state of *being*.

But the problem is our familiarity, family, upbringing, training, friends, and culture. Everyone and everything point us toward having or doing. All the commercial industries sell having and doing for *being*. "Come to our store and purchase this piece of clothing, and you will be happy." Millions and millions of unnecessary articles get sold every second. Because of that mind mistake, the idea of *having* something, we believe that *having* is the same as *being* and that we will be happy. Or in the window of the travel agency, you are enticed to take a trip to a perfect island. You imagine how you could be, always paired with a picture of the perfect sandy beach and a deeply tanned woman in perfect physical proportions and condition.

Again, advertising companies sell us the illusion of happiness, all because we still don't understand "having and doing" has nothing to do with being. Basically, each of us agreed with different conditioning for our being, which varies from person to person. But truly these are our personal, familiar, and cultural conditions. We have trained ourselves to have some requirements for our being. Imagine a perfect sunny day on a dreamlike sandy beach, like the poster advertising an island vacation. We create a situation with all possible entertainments and all kinds of food and drinks and invite dozens of people to this "be happy" party.

We would observe lots of disagreement about what one should do to be happy. Some want to play while the others want to swim, drink, or eat. Not necessarily a few agree with playing. Would they also agree with the game they'd like to play? Even if they agree to play cards, they would not agree on a card game. Maybe some decide not to do anything. They'd just lie down and listen to music and then have all kinds of delicious food and drink. Still at the end of the day, we will hear excuses why some couldn't be completely happy.

One may say, "There was enough to eat, but because I was on a diet, I couldn't eat." Another may say, "I ate too much. I don't fit in my swimsuit. If I lose some weight, then I can be happy."

We hear all kinds of statements every day as to why someone's not happy. This goes back to his or her personal requirement for happiness. What is said here is not about having different options from which to choose. What is said here is that, in order to enter the domain of *being*, we don't necessarily need to pass through the alternate domain of "having and doing." In today's world of astronomically growing supply and demand in all different directions, we face lots of changes and doubts about which choices we have to make. Therefore, everyone has developed a very specific way of how one should handle, give and take, perform, and maneuver through these two planes of "having and doing."

Have you tried recently to order coffee in a coffee shop? This task comes with lots of specifications like tall, short, or grande; double or single shot; caffeinated or not; dozens of different flavors; no milk or sugar; and so on.

It's not so much about a cup of tea or coffee. It's about the mind-set behind the cup of tea, the mind of requirement, expectation, or automatic cultural influences that make that experience pleasant or painful or easy or complicated. To prepare a cup of tea is not so difficult. You need hot water, loose tea or a tea bag, and a cup. There is a cartoon called "Oriental or Western Tea."

First, Mr. Westerner visited Mr. Oriental where he was asked if he would like a cup of tea. Mr. Westerner agreed then. Water was heated, two cups came out of the cupboard, and loose tea was brewed into a teapot. The tea was poured into the cups, followed with enjoyable conversation and laughter. Then the visit was over.

Next time Mr. Oriental visited Mr. Westerner in his home. He was asked if he desired a cup of tea. This was followed by many other questions: What kind of tea? With caffeine or without? Loose tea or a tea bag? Do you like it strong or weak? Would you like a mug or a tea glass?

Eventually Mr. Oriental was overwhelmed with all the questions and said, "I don't care. Just make it the way that you like, and that will be okay."

Mr. Westerner started to brew the tea. But he was not through with the tea questions and continued to ask, "Where do you prefer to sit with your tea: Inside or outside on the balcony? Sitting at the table or on the couch? Would you like the sunny side or the shade? Shall we have tea with open or half-open window?"

Now Mr. Oriental's voice was not gentle or soft any longer. It was rough and loud. "Can you just stop asking thousands of questions and just make the tea? We'll sit wherever."

Mr. Westerner, totally disappointed, replied, "I just want to make you the perfect cup of tea, like we had at your place."

Of course, it's nice to have choices, but we should remember that, every time we are choosing one over another, we are creating another requirement in the plane of "having and doing." Ultimately, we choose in order to become happy, and we forget that, with every step we make toward being happy, there was a half-step toward the opposite side, not being happy.

This half-step is hidden, and we don't see it until we get far enough away to recognize it. If we head far enough toward the west, we find ourselves in the east. With every step toward the west, it was a hidden half-step toward the east. The shift becomes clear only if we go far enough to accumulate all the hidden opposite half-steps.

With every choice that we make, we let go of some of our flexibility. We forget how gradually we lose our flexibility and get more specific and rigid. If we observe a little stream of water that is flowing over a mountain, when that little stream reaches a piece of rock, because the water is flexible, it eventually goes to the left, right, below, or above the rock.

What we learn from this observation is, if we had to make a choice, we had better choose our flexibility over anything else because, when we are flexible, we flow. Flexibility makes the way. It's not that the little stream chose left or right. The flow and the choice are one, as if they have met one another halfway.

Masters have been teaching this truth when they say, "By dropping our attachments to the outcomes and flowering our acceptance and faith, we reach a point where the universe unfolds, and we embrace whatever comes. It becomes a synchronized dance rather than a situation of stress and pursuit and moments of unclear decision-making.

Lots of requirements and specifications for happiness leads to disappointments, frustrations, and unhappiness. If we want to be happy, we need to learn to *be*. If we want to enjoy our *being*, we should learn to be flexible and embrace the unfolding universe.

We have all seen people who constantly struggle to make choices, and sometimes it becomes so hard for them to choose between what appears in front of them that they may reach out for some advice. People who are in the flow look like they are not making any choices at all. The half-wise have to make choices all the time; the wise ones only make a few. The enlightened ones flow and don't need to make choices because the options on the path unfold themselves. They are synchronized with the flow, while the abandoned ones cut off the road they're on and choose another one.

Gratitude Meditation

Brew a cup of tea and find a quiet place, ideally in a garden or in nature, where you are not distracted by anyone or a ringing phone. Select a place where you can sit with your cup of tea and know it is your time.

Mindfully, before taking your first sip, give thanks to the tea, cup, and your hand holding it, along with the place you are sitting in and the time. While you are enjoying your tea, contemplate with every new sip, and try to follow the journey the tea has taken before it landed in your teacup.

Give thanks to the shop where you got the tea and all the workers who were involved in that transaction.

Give thanks to all the drivers and people who make the delivery to the shop possible.

Give thanks to the ship and its crew involved in the cruise trip.

Give thanks to the drivers and people who made the delivery to the ship and all the middlemen.

Give thanks to the factory and workers who cleaned and packed the tea.

Give thanks to everyone who helped the delivery of the tea to the factory.

Give thanks to all the workers and people who were harvesting and picking the tea leaves.

Give thanks to the farmers and their families who grew the tea.

Give thanks to plants, pollinators, and the land.

Give thanks to the rain and rain makers that nourished the tea planting.

You can perform this same mediation with bread.

Priorities

We all hear many critical comments from people that we live with. Most of their complaints are about the environment and time. One may say, "I don't have time for vacation … I don't have time to create art … I don't have time for mediation."

Let us look at those kinds of statements more closely. Can an artist have no time for creating art? Can a musician say he doesn't have time to make music? Can someone who has found the most precious jewels of meditation say she has no time for meditation"

The statement "I don't have time" is not exactly correct. We always have time. In fact, we are *living* time. A friend said he loved fishing, and after a while, he said he wished to go back to fishing soon. And then a little later, he said he had not been fishing in years. Is it possible that someone has no time for his interest, passion, or calling? The truth is, consciously or subconsciously, we divide time to fractions, which makes the base and foundation for our activities. This division and segmentation depend on where we put the anchor of priorities. Priorities get replaced all the time throughout our life. As a teenager, if our priority were to go dancing, it may shift later on to listening to music, visiting friends, or even having quiet time with ourselves.

The priority shift may occur naturally or be forced on us politically, socially, or environmentally. The forced shift that makes us change our lifestyle and priority is sometimes so subtle that we may not notice it, and we may think we changed our priority of our own free will. But after examining the nature of the change mindfully, we will recognize the truth of it.

The truth behind the priority change for the friend who didn't go fishing for years in the above example was one of environmental force. He explained that his company changed his work schedule, and the day he usually had off for fishing had gone away.

When there is a political shift where we are living now, the echo of that shift may vibrate through your housing situation and even your home ownership status. You may even be forced to change your lifestyle and therefore your priorities. These are the extreme shifts and noticeable, but the forced shifts in the daily life are subtle and not recognizable. We never notice how many adjustments we need to make to deal with the gradual monetary inflation of the costs of everything. These necessary adjustments directly or indirectly change our priorities. We also have to sacrifice a lot for all these forced shifts. These necessary and sometimes unnecessary adjustments we make change our priorities list. Sometimes they shift so dramatically that the list becomes reversed. For example, our *well-being*, which should be our first priority, gets buried underneath so-called obligations and lots of objects, houses, cars, furniture, and so on.

Just before departure on an airplane, flight attendants remind us, in the case of an emergency, we need to take care of ourselves first. Even if there is a life-threatening situation, like a pressure change in the cabin, we need to first put the oxygen mask on ourselves and secondly on the children or infants. This reminder shows us again where the priority should be. All the other priorities should remain underneath our well-being. In modern life, most people lose their heath because of the forced shift of their priorities. Because of the inhumane "civilization" rules, the first priority of all, our well-being, gets neglected, and our lives get put in danger.

There is no doubt that we need to be flexible with the changes, have no rigid opinion about our lifestyle, and not to persist on our priorities, but the point is to recognize the difference between when our priorities change contemplatively and freely or when we are pushed to alter them. It's all about becoming more aware of the enforced and external shove, for example, the invasion of our privacy, which modern life is totally guilty of. Something that is inadequate, impolite, and even rude suddenly becomes *lawful*, and we become a part of that.

In the last few years, video cameras have been installed everywhere.

They're installed in the hallways, lobbies, and airports, all for security reasons. Not only are they at major intersections, they're on the highways and in every bus, rail, and gas station we all visit. Cameras are fixed on our face in most every store where we buy things. They're on rail and subways cars, and this chain reaction has changed the face of our society so much that we even have video cameras on our portable phones.

No one must ask your permission for your photo or a video of you anymore. Can you guess how many times a day you are captured on video each day? While you are driving, visiting shopping centers, buying your groceries, entering your office building or your sport club, or whatever you do, it's no longer about video during travel. It's moving toward watching everyday life. The direct force of all these and even the side effects forces us into new changes, alterations that directly affect our lifestyles and turn our priorities upside down.

If we forget the importance of our priorities and try to deepen our understanding to see what our priority at the time of being, we always come back to the simple truth that to just *be* should be and remain our priority. It's a necessity for our spiritual, psychological, emotional, and physical well-being to touch base with our being every day. Many of us have never experienced being completely present.

Being present, totally and completely, is more than the physical appearances. It's more than talking or communicating. It's more than *doing* something or *having* something. Just *being* is a complete state by itself. It doesn't need any additions. If we add something to that complete state, it becomes incomplete. Unnecessary additions brought to the complete state of *being* come from our busy minds. We can face our busy mind every time we seek quietness, silent moments, meditation time, or retreats.

We speak two ways, inside of ourselves and outside to the external world. The second one is very familiar to us. The first one is even more familiar than the second one, but we are not supposed to talk about it because of the fear of being labeled. The truth is that we speak *in* all the time, but most of the time silently. The mind that speaks *in* has been recognized in many cultures and traditions.

Masters remind us that, when we are faced by a challenging situation or problem, the inner chatter gets more active, resulting in a busy mind. What is the medicine here? The medicine is to go for refuge in our being, even if it's harder to go there when we are challenged. By every attempt, with each silent practice or meditation, we see we have reduced the busyness of our mind. The beautiful saying, "If you find yourself in a hole, stop digging," reminds us that, when the inner chatter is most active, it is the time to stop and not be afraid or concerned about this "inner chatter," but just to watch it.

We need to realize the simple truth: we don't need to engage in all the conversations that the inner chatter brings with itself. Many times, when we think that we are thinking, it is actually the inner chatter talking to us. Because the inner chatter is so fast, we miss the step between it and thinking. To be only a watcher or an observer is a great way to reduce our thoughts.

Masters guide us to the understanding that life is an experience. If we accept the flow of life with all its ups and downs, just enjoying the ride, it becomes a unique and pleasant experience. If we start to judge, judge the flow, get critical, worry about its downs, and try to cling to its ups, it becomes a painful experience. The painful experience elevates itself into a nightmare if we try to control life. The flow of life cannot be controlled because it's not stationary, ridged, or constant.

Masters who have gone very deep in their meditation to experience the principle of that flow brought back to us the knowledge of how to cope with that ever-flowing life. The principle is to rotate and regulate. To understand how it applies to operating the vehicle of life, we can look at how we drive our own cars. If we only rotate (use the gas pedal), we may cause lots of accidents. Regulation is the various tiny and sometimes major adjustments that we make with the steering wheel and brakes. Sometimes we need to only focus on regulating and temporarily forget about rotating. We may do this with the brake, applying gentle braking action or coming to a complete stop.

Balance is the stillness; counterbalance is the movement. We can observe this when a juggler spins a plate on the end of his or her finger, how the tiny adjustments of the movement create the balance of the plate. In order to get the maximum potential of energy, we always need a counterbalance. Rotation and regulation are balance and counterbalance to one another.

Unfortunately, we know only one mode, to rotate. Because of the hypnotic effect of rotation on us from one side and the attachment to the new illusionary identification to objects and events on the path of rotation on the other side, this make us continue to rotate without any, or just a tiny bit, of regulation, which is not enough for the balance and counterbalance principle. Soon we get lopsided, get out of balance, lose lots of flexibility, and create more stress and anxiety. We create more stress and anxiety in ourselves, resulting in frustration, anger, and fear.

The natural process of the principle of rotation and regulation can be observed throughout nature. If we go hiking in the woods, we see lots of trees growing together. If a tree is growing and growing (rotating) and suddenly notices that the neighboring tree is coming into its path, it puts the gear into regulation and starts to make space for the other tree. We may not see this at first glance, but we observe deeply that truth throughout seasons and even at the level of the universe. Mostly the regulations are the tiny or major adjustments that we make in our inner world. If we are content in our inner world, the outer world, satisfaction, happiness, joy, and ease becomes a natural by-product. We always exude what we are feeling inside of us.

If something bad happens to a close relative or friend, the moment that he or she arrives at our door, we get to understand that something is not quite right. On occasion, we need to regulate in the external world, but mostly it is an inner matter.

Priorities Meditation

Find a quiet place where you can be for a while without any external distractions. You may choose to listen to gentle nature music. Rainfall or ocean waves are perfect. Very mindfully burn a candle and incense, placing them a few feet from where you are seated.

Ideally, we want to create a place where the sun is not directly shining on the candle and incense. Rather a shaft of sunlight shines behind the smoke, allowing you to watch the smoke to rise and dance though the light beam. If a shaft of sunlight is not available, place the candle near the incense, allowing the heat of the flame to pull the column of smoke toward it.

As you are watching the dancing incense smoke, notice how your thoughts are getting lighter and disappearing. Observe this for a while. Notice how your rising thoughts and the dancing smoke are synchronized. If you are listening to nature music, notice how the music and dancing smoke are synchronized. Enjoy all this synchronicity until all your thoughts disappear but only the hypnotic smoke dances in the candle flame remain. Meditate on this dance, until you become the dance.

Sit so long until you feel all the necessary and unnecessary priorities have dissolved into your being.

PRIORITIES

Time

The most common word in the English language—and perhaps in other languages as well—is *time*. Because of that reason alone, we should check in to see whether time has more than one meaning. Before we tap into the various meanings of time, let's see if we can find the most common meanings of the word *time*.

The most common interpretation of time is something that is external and mechanical, so mechanical that we can even measure it. That is why we use clocks, watches, and all kinds of timers, such as day minders, weekly and monthly planners, and calendars. This kind of mechanical time is rigid and very local. That's why, for example, 4:00 p.m. at the place where you are reading this book is not 4:00 p.m. all over the planet. And it may vary from 4:00 p.m. to 12:00 p.m. or even 12:00 a.m. according to which direction, east or west, you go.

This mechanical time is the foundation of every modern society. Probably in every modern society, people start their workday at 8:00 a.m. or earlier in the morning, and they finish at 5:00 p.m. or later in the afternoon. When we go to work, we may see our boss or eventually work with the boss at the same office. The boss cannot be with us all the time. But, his agents, the timekeepers, are everywhere. Not only at the office, but also in our houses.

The boss is not personally in our bedroom to shout "Get up!" but his agent, the alarm clock, is. Its ringing or beeping might ruin the best dream ever or the most delicious moment in bed. We leap out of bed and get ready to go because the next challenge is not going to wait for us. The next challenge could be taking the bus or the person who is taking us to work. Our driver cannot wait for us because he or she has to race as well, and he or she needs to compete with his or her time too. Each and every one of us has another schedule and another race, and no one can stop his or her race because someone else is late. If you are late, it means that you couldn't manage your race properly. And you have lost one or some of your races.

Because this kind of time is mechanical and rigid, there would be no negotiation possible with any agent of time. As we mentioned, this creation and interpretation of mechanical time is artificial and man-made. It was designed in a way that either your boss or one of his agents, the timekeepers, are watching you all the time. Timekeepers have been spread throughout your entire life. This agent is like active cancer cells going to every social place, to all of the meetings and gatherings. They are all over your living space. They have entered your bedroom on some occasion. They may even stop you from getting a good night's sleep. Or they may even cause you a sleepless night because of the staff meeting scheduled for the next morning. This scheduling sometimes goes so far that we eat when we are not hungry or don't eat when we *are* hungry because it is not lunch*time*. We may even postpone our needs to go to the restroom.

Now the question is: why did we create this artificial time? Before opening this question, let us look at time from nature's point of view and operation. What happens if we put some seeds in the garden at our house, making sure they receive enough care, water, and sunshine? According to what we sow, we may harvest, and eventually we may observe some buds appearing, which will develop into flowers. Do seeds have timers? Clocks? What about the sunshine? Does the sun carry a watch? When the flowers have reached their peak, their most beautiful and fragrant state, we might put them in a vase to admire them in our house. But deep inside, we know they will change and fade away.

Why do flowers fade away? Do they have a timer to know when it's time to go? If they have a timer, where do they hide it? We may make a list of such questions, but the truth is that all these types of questions appear because of our fundamental mistake of interpretation of time. Time has a flow of ripening, becoming, aging, and fading away. Like the buds that turn into flowers, they become fragrant and beautiful, flowers that we put on the table and enjoy. The flowers offer their beauty and fragrance to existence where they came from. And after a while, they fade away and go back home. Everything is circulating in the infinite cycle of coming and going, appearing and disappearing, rising and ceasing, so-called "birth" and "death."

These cycles have nothing to do with the watches on our hands. Both cycles, of seeds becoming flowers in our gardens and maintaining them on the table in our house, could have been altered by changing environmental conditions. In other words, with a little change in our care and an amount of sunshine, the flowers will have fallen into another cycle of existence.

All of the possible cycles that the flower may have chosen have something in common. They all were organic and flexible, compared to mechanical and rigid clock-time. By the same token, if there is a time, how long is the human life span? We all know that every individual goes through different cycles. No one can say anything about the individual cycles.

There are people who depart to go back home as a baby, toddler, teenager, adult, or at a very old age according to their cycles, and no one knows about any human's departure time. This graduation and going back home by completing their cycles has nothing to do with any ticking on any clock on any wall. This graduation depends entirely on the individual. It depends on how and when he or she completes his or her lessons, how he or she finishes his or her earthwork. Has this person completed and passed his or her final test to go back home, to Source, or shall he or she face another cycle of existence?

How human beings came to assume all these organic and flexible seasons and organic human life as something rigid and dynamic goes back to the intellectual mind. The intellectual mind likes to measure everything and compare that measurement to something else. That's why we measure how short, tall, narrow, or wide something might be. The way the intellectual mind works is the following: measure it, stick a label on it, and put it in a box. And now you know it.

What happens if we go to a party where we don't know anyone but the host? We will be asked many questions by everyone: What is your name? How do you know the host? What do you do? Where do you live? All of these questions are asked so their intellectual mind can find a box for us to be placed in, allowing them to think they know us.

Anyway, the intellectual mind likes to know things. That's why it needs a beginning and an end to everything. Now, between the beginning and the end, there are many degrees of measurement for this mind.

Another thing the intellectual mind likes is to localize and freeze things. For example, we are talking about a friend, and the information passed to us was that the friend is middle-aged. This fact is not enough to satisfy the mind. It wants to go further and pinpoint the friend with some numbers. That's why the more localized, the more rigid, and the more numerated, the better for the intellectual mind.

Now, go back to the different cycles that flowers both in the garden and on the table would have chosen. Each option would have been organic and flexible. In other words, within the different cycles, time would have expanded and contracted. That's exactly what time is doing. Contraction and expansion create an organic flow.

This organic flow of existence is unique and different in each stage of life. Every stage of life has another span and flow, another rate of passing through. Albert Einstein said, "Put your hand on a hot stove for a minute, and it seems like an hour. Sit with a pretty girl for an hour, and it seems like a minute." It doesn't have the same flow. One goes very slow and painful, while the other flies gently and gracefully. And every other activity we may choose is somewhere in between.

Time is happening at different rates and span and flow in different streams of life—so different streams, illusions, scenarios, and appearances. They are all unique and fresh. Can you remember an occasion when mechanical time totally surprised you by passing much faster than you actually thought? Each of us has lots of examples of these memories. All of us have experienced visiting a close friend when the conversation is lively and fond memories are shared. Highlights are remembered by one, and the other continues with the story. The one friend finishes the sentence of the other. Suddenly one is totally shocked by checking the time and seeing that hours have flown by on the mechanical timer.

In this kind of situation, we get the experience that we were in another flow of time, or if you are a time-oriented person, you would say, "We were in another time *zone*."

This is not so much about what word we use, flow versus time zone or cycles and seasons versus time and timing. It is all about understanding that one is flexible, organic, and alive and the other is dynamic and rigid. One is alive and is contracting, expanding, and flowing, while the other one is mechanical and a repetition of the same unit. Even more important than finding out if time is organic or rigid is to realize where the entrance or the gateway to that dimension is.

Unfortunately, we cannot write or read about the truth of the dimension that we call time. There is no way to show its gateway to anyone. That truth can only be revealed to us through the individual experience.

Fortunately, we can all experience that truth through the upcoming "Time Meditation." Have a nice journey, and welcome to the time-free zone.

Time Meditation

Sit quietly in a comfortable place where you can be for a while without any distraction. Find a comfortable position and contemplate,

> I am living on a planet where everything gets measured in order to fit in a box. The biggest box that has been created on this planet is called "time." I am sitting here to experience the truth of time. I understand what we call "past" is an aspect or the infinite possibilities and dimensions of the now. I also understand what we call "future" is another aspect or dimension of the now. Where these dimensions are, I don't know, but I know without my being operating in the now that none of these dimensions could be explored or experienced.

Next, call any event you wish from the past. Go through all the details and focus on the emotions rising out of that journey. Live that experience until you are suddenly dropped back into your being and notice you are sitting in the now.

Next, recall any plan for the future and start the journey. Go through as many of the details as you can and let yourself go through the emotional roller coaster with all of its ups and downs until you notice you are sitting in the meditation.

Continue to contemplate: Did my being truly go through the past or future, or was I really just sitting here and didn't go anywhere? Either way, the key to unlock any dimension, "past" or "future," is in the now.

The now is the gateway to all dimensions; therefore, the being who lives in the now could be multidimensional. Meditate on your timeless multidimensionality as long as your body allows you before rising up out of the meditation.

Appendix

To Touch Base with the Source

How often do we touch base with our foundation, meaning to find a quiet time, sit in the sunshine, and connect with our surroundings to the trees, birds, and sky? Watch butterflies. See how gently they fly and carry their beauty to the flowers. Observe how the wind blows through the trees and carries the pollen through the air to further green life. See how insects make different homes and make music while they fly. Experience how our feet touch the warm sand, the moist grass, or solid rock and how they exchange their electromagnetism with Mother Earth, giving away fatigue and receiving life. How often do we have a genuine and honest healing talk with our higher self or the Great Spirit?

Now that we have gone through all the great messages in this book and know how to meditate, let us do this last meditation very sincerely and faithfully.

Touching Base with the Source Meditation

When you are ready, we'll touch base with our source, Great Spirit, God, The All, Universal Parent, or whatever name you have for the Source. Tell the Great Spirit, "As a human being, living in this space time, we are always worried about the future. Therefore, I am sitting here humbly, to touch base with the truth, with a quest. Is the universe, Great Spirit, going to provide and take care of this child in the future, or would I only be on my own?"

Sit long enough in meditation until you are touched by the spirit or you've got the answer, even if it should take some time. Usually there is an immediate answer. After we have been touched and have been given an answer, we may doubt it and ask ourselves: was it an answer from above, or are we making something up and claiming our thoughts as being holy?

These doubts and questions rise from our ego. The ego doesn't want us to be connected with our higher self or whatever we call that existential power. The ego wants to draw our attention to itself. Masters who are in alignment with the universal energy don't feel that kind of separation any longer. They don't ask which thoughts are my thoughts and which are from the Source. They don't ask the question: am I resonating with the higher universal vibrations, or am I hallucinating? Their thoughts and the universal thoughts, the universal intelligence, and the existential energy have become one. They are so in alignment with the universe that nothing can separate their thoughts from the existential energy. These all happen when we put away our ego and we don't go with the attitude of "my way or the highway" because there is only one way and that's "the way." This is most likely the meaning of the Tao.

Imagine a normal human body. If we are, for example, a cell in the liver, if we come to the point that we call it enlightenment, suddenly we wake up and realize, "Oh! I am a tiny cell in the liver." No, we suddenly see ourselves, our liver, our body, the room that we are sitting in, and … We understand the big, big body, the universe. We are suddenly connected to everything and all times. We are one with all our ancestors who have graduated before us. And then at this moment, there is no before or after, that moment holds all time, that which we call before, past, after, or future.

Suddenly, that spot that we are sitting at becomes the entire universe, holding every space that we've been in before and every space that we may visit later on. We understand the true meaning of the word *connection* because we get connected to all spaces and all time and we get awake.

Buddha Shakyamuni sat under a banyan tree for seven years until he saw the light of enlightenment. After enlightenment, people asked him, "Are you God now?"

He replied, "No."

They asked him, "Are you a prophet?"

"No."

"Are you a sage, a holy being, a rishi, a rabbi, or a leader now?"

"No."

"Then are you still a human being? Who are you then?"

He replied, "I am awake,"

The "awakened one" is what "Buddha" means. When we get awake and see that we are in the eternal moment of now, we will get connected to all beings, connected to all time. We understand we don't need to be worried about anything in the future. And we don't need to regret anything about the past because what is tangible and real is only the present moment. But in our minds, we create linear time to hold past, present moment, and future in that order.

We glue everything together. We glue the day before yesterday with yesterday and today with tomorrow and the day after tomorrow, and so we create a rigid linear time. By doing this, we don't realize how the present moment is like a very slippery fish that jumped out of our hands. Life is happening while we are planning to eventually get to a life. The present moment has passed while we are either in the past or the future.

And unfortunately, not even that happens. We are not even in the past or the future. We were in the present moment but didn't realize it or use it. Because we separate ourselves from the rest of the universe and listen to our ego, we start to have the feeling of possession and fear. The moment we start to feel "I possess this and that," we also create the fear of losing it.

Yes, we create our scarecrows. Once a master said, "A thought of possession creates ten thousand scarecrows, and each scarecrow is attached to ten thousand thoughts of possession." The moment we think that our car is more than a vehicle to move us around and we start to develop a feeling of possession, we will eventually create many thoughts of fear about losing that possession. The same story goes for all other objects that are here to bring ease and comfort, but they actually bring us anxiety and fear.

There is a battle of protecting them that feeds our fear of losing them. We continue to exaggerate this behavior so long until possessions shine and become the source of our happiness and joy. When that happens, we are really in trouble because we have developed a very strong attachment to these objects. Recently many people in the United States committed suicide. They thought because of the momentary bad economy that they would be unable to pay their mortgage, and some of them thought that, if they lost their house, they had lost their source of happiness and joy.

They didn't see that the cause of their happiness didn't lie in an external object. The cause of their happiness was inside of them, and they were in trouble not because of the bad economy, but because of their attachment that had been developed through years of practice. We can manifest every thought if we exercise that thought long enough.

Throughout life, we meet people who exercise a fear thought or a misfortune thought for so long that one day the manifestation of that thought is in front of them. They scream and shout, "I knew that! I knew that! I knew one day it would happen!" They forget that they were creating that event by exercising that thought over and over again, so long that the universe had to give it to them.

Ask, and you shall receive. Whatsoever and whatever we ask, we shall receive, good or bad things. We forget that "good" or "bad" is *our* definition and they have nothing to do with reality. Things just are, but we differentiate them according to our culture and upbringing. We categorize them as "good" or "bad."

When we call a sickness to us that is bad for us but good for the bacteria or viruses or germs, the universe or God doesn't tell us, "Wait a second! You are asking for something that is not good for you; therefore I'm not giving that to you."

If that would be the case, what happens with our freedom and our free will? We have been given the power to create things. We are co-creators. We have the free will to choose our path and create things. We can create sicknesses or the path to enlightenment. Thoughts are nothing but electromagnetic waves. Every thought can be tapped into at any given time or situation. But it's much easier to tap into the thoughts that are already presented to us by people, situations, and environment.

If we go to church, temple, mosque, or any place of worship, it's much easier to capture religious or philosophical thoughts and sometimes more peaceful or essential thoughts. If we go for a walk on a summer afternoon to a green area with lots of trees and birds, it's more likely that we will feel more relaxed. Peaceful and relaxed thoughts will merge into our mind.

But if we listen to any kind of news media, it's more likely that we get negative thoughts because mostly news is about economic or social battles and catastrophes. It doesn't mean that we never get a single negative thought when we go for a walk or hiking to a beautiful place. It only means that the possibility for negative thoughts are less in nature than if we engage in a conversation with a friend after seeing a horror movie. That's why nature has been stretching its arms and hands to us, to go there and get that vibration, that peace and tranquility.

Trees, flowers, lakes, grass, and birds, generally nature, is waiting for us so we can resonate with their vibration. When we watch animals—kittens, puppies, or neighborhood birds—or other animals, we start to feel their simplicity and innocence. We get the feeling that they are not as complicated as human beings. They don't have any thoughts of future as we human beings do. Even though if they are gathering food for winter, they are doing this naturally and purely, and there is no concern about selling them later for a profit or being in control of the market. They do this instinctively and naturally.

If we touch base frequently with the Source and recognize who we really are, suddenly all the layers and dimensions that we go through become alive and meaningful. Not only does our life become meaningful, so does our death. How to embrace the flower of death can be understood in one of the greatest stories in Sufism, the story of the merchant and the dervish. The dervish is someone who has given up all the worldly possessions and values and has chosen the path of detachment for spiritual growth and enlightenment.

> A famous merchant in his finest silk robe with his entourage were passing through the bazaar and collecting all the attention and respect from the people. He became furious when he noticed a dervish passing his crew without paying them any of the extra attention that he expected. The following dialog between the merchant and the dervish is worthwhile to keep in our treasured memory.

Merchant: Don't you see who's walking here (showing his noble silk robe)?

Dervish: I saw you even before you entered the bazaar.

Merchant: If you are seeing us (again showing his noble silk robe), why aren't you paying us any respect?

Dervish: Of course I'm paying respect to all creation, but maybe in a way you are not familiar with.

Merchant: Are you trying to educate us? Don't you see who's here before you? Don't you see who *you* are (pointing to the dervish's simple, worn-out robe)? You are worthless, and if you could see yourself, you would see it's better to die right now.

Dervish: I can see my true self; therefore I have no attachment to any form of my being and could embrace death at any time. What about you?

Merchant: (bursting into sarcastic laughter, turning toward his servants, and pointing toward the dervish) He says he can die at any time. (Looking back at the dervish) Can you die *now*?

Dervish: Meaninglessly, no. But if my death can bring some fruit of knowledge or any teaching to this moment, yes.

Merchant: Here is the deal, if you don't die now, you go to the end of the line of my servants. But if you truly die now, I will become *your* servant. No, that's impossible because you will be dead, so I will become the servant of your path of detachment and give all my wealth to the poor.

Upon hearing this, the dervish kissed the ground, laid down, took off his worn-out sandals, placed them as a pillow under his head, and breathed his last breath. Completely in … and out …

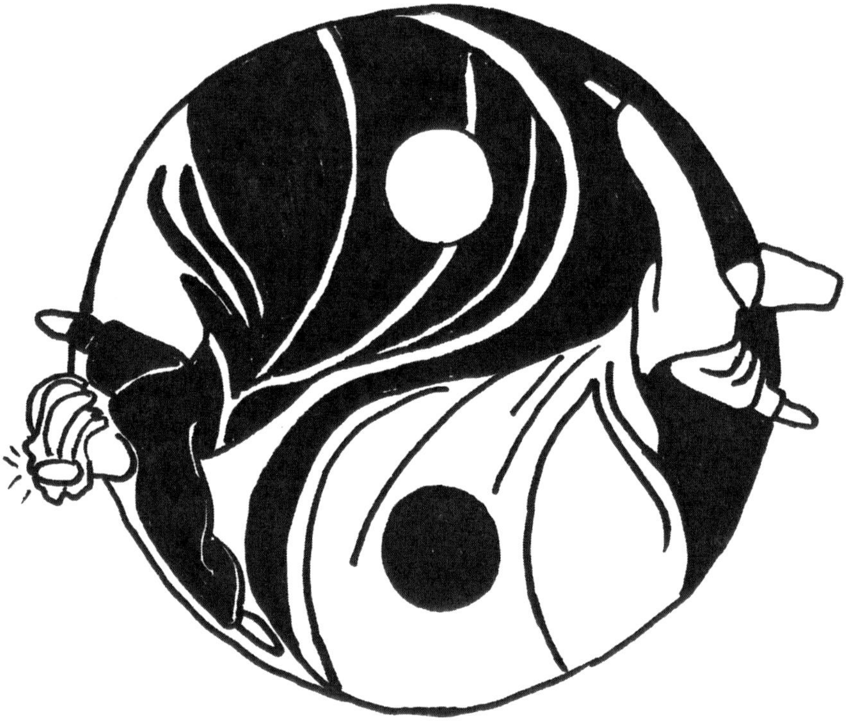

Glossary

Awareness

Direct perceiver; direct apprehending.
    Generally, awareness is divided into two kinds of awareness: sense awareness and mental awareness. Sense awareness is of seeing and hearing sounds, along with experiencing odors, taste, and touch. Mental awareness is the direct perceiver.

Being, The Being

A living thing; a human being; a person.

Blessing

Transformation of the state of being or an object from negative to positive through the inspiration of a Holy Being or simply through the grace of existence.

Buddha

A being who has reached the state of Nirvana; the complete abandonment of all the delusions and imprints.
    Many beings have reached this state in the past. There are some Buddhas among us now, and there will be many who will become Buddha in times to come.

Chi

Also written as "Qi"; the life force that governs the entire universe.

The foglike or even transparent chi around us is not recognized by our visual awareness, but if we move our hand mindfully and very slowly, the layers of chi can be received and stored in our hands and can be transmitted through our beings. Qi-gung masters and martial artists have been using, applying, and transmuting this life force for centuries. Also see Universal Energy.

Conscientiousness

A nonmaterial factor with two natural tendencies attracting and flowing toward what is virtuous and letting go and detaching itself from any delusion and non-virtue.

Dervish

A disciple of the path of detachment; someone who has detached from the material world and has embraced the non-attachment path for the purpose of spiritual awakening and enlightenment.

Disciple

A determined student of the spiritual path.

Earthwork

Going through the layers of being a disciple and the mastery; all the learning, experiences, and teaching; accumulating the lessons and putting them into application; going through all ups and downs and finally getting ready for graduation.

Ecstasy

The transformational feeling of a being from a negative to a positive state, from weakness and unhappiness to strength or joyfulness.

Existence

The whole universe, including all their beings, seen and unseen, of any realm of reality.

Enlightenment

Liberation; liberation through unification of the opposites; getting liberated from grasping at inherent existence from the dreamlike state of conventional truth and becoming a direct perceiver of the true nature of the phenomena and existence.

Entropy

Decline; deterioration; breaking down.

Great Spirit

The Spirit behind all creation.

Guru

A qualified spiritual teacher and guide; one who can guide the disciple along and through his or her spiritual path.

Healing Energy

The higher and highest vibration of the universal energy that can be received and transmitted; known as Pranic and spiritual energies.

Inner Chatter

The vibration and frequency and its formation inside in the form of thoughts and speech.

Inner Court

The domain of the intellectual mind, where everything, everyone, and every event gets evaluated, classified, and judged.

Inner Space

The domain in which the conventional nature of phenomena has been converted to the true nature of the phenomena; the self.

Master

Generally, anyone who has reached the level of the mastery in his or her field; spiritual beings and teachers who have seen the light of enlightenment.

Meditation

Concentration and focus of wisdom that allows the mind to focus like a laser and tie itself to an object of meditation.

Mindfulness

A type of wisdom that allows the mind to focus on the object of meditation or tie itself to a virtuous object.

Omnipresent

Being aware and present in all the layers of the illusion of time and space.

Phenomenon; Pl. Phenomena

Generally, any fact or event that can be observable; particularly any ordinary or extraordinary object of awareness.

Present Moment

The eternal moment of now with no beginning and no end.

Pure Consciousness

In general, the unmanifested, transparent, and raw material for the makeup of the universe.
    In particular, a person of the desire realm, like the human being, is an aggregate of manifested pure consciousness in the form of physical body, thoughts, emotions and mind, and the spark of unmanifested pure consciousness.

Rishi

"Seers"; sage; one who went to deep meditation, realizing the true nature of phenomena; guru.

Sage

One who is distinguished, recognized, or honored for wisdom.

Self

The conventional nature of a phenomenon that is based on matter and survival.

Spirit

The energy behind matter that allows and unleashes the physical manifestation.

Generally, *every* object (including animals, plants, and humans) consist of two kinds of energy: matter energy and spirit energy. Matter energy has been manifested in the form of its particular object, but the unmanifested spirit energy of the object, the part that is not unleashed to matter energy, stays formless and unseen. Many religions have the belief that only human beings are linked to the spirit energy. Objects, plants, and animals have been discriminated from spirit energy. Human beings, a very recent arrival in the evolutionary chain, interpret love and compassion from animals as only instinctual behavior.

SPIRITUAL WANDERING

A wandering dedicated to the spiritual awakening and growth, usually done with a physical and mental diet where the disciples have no food or possessions with them on the journey.

The disciples put away their intellectual mind prior to the period of wandering.

TAO

Literally means "the way"; the path.

The teaching of the mystical philosophy is the religion linked to Taoism, which is Taoist mystical philosophy intertwined with Buddhism.

THE SELF

The true nature of the phenomena that is based on the highest cosmic vibration and frequency.

TRANSCENDING

Generally, levitation of any kind, particularly allowing the primitive and raw mind to get the experience of higher levels of the universal knowledge.

UNIVERSAL ENERGY

The endless Chi around and within everything.
 Generally everything in the universe is made of and is part of the universal energy.

UNIVERSAL INTELLIGENCE

Generally, the intelligence around and within all the phenomena; in particular the concentrated and focused intelligence of all the phenomena.

Index

A

acceptance 92
age 81, 105
alchemical 8
anger 4, 5, 10, 24, 73, 82, 99
attachment 36, 64, 66, 99, 114, 116, 120
attention viii, 15, 26, 27, 41, 55, 77, 81, 112, 115
awareness 7, 25, 26, 27, 63, 64, 73, 119, 120, 123

B

being 1, 2, 3, 4, 5, 8, 11, 19, 26, 30, 32, 36, 38, 40, 43, 44, 45, 52, 53, 55, 57, 58, 60, 63, 64, 65, 66, 69, 72, 74, 76, 78, 79, 82, 83, 85, 87, 88, 89, 90, 91, 92, 96, 97, 100, 108, 111, 112, 115, 116, 119, 120, 121, 123
belief 2, 9, 19, 124
belief system 9, 19
Big Bang 23, 26
birth 7, 27, 35, 66, 105
blessing 21, 23, 47, 119
bliss 5, 73
blissful 89
body 1, 3, 10, 19, 23, 26, 27, 32, 40, 41, 49, 55, 59, 60, 63, 65, 76, 108, 112, 123
breathing 26, 32, 55, 60, 63
Buddha 49, 112, 119

C

ceremonies viii
ceremony 18
change 7, 11, 17, 19, 25, 32, 49, 54, 57, 59, 73, 76, 77, 84, 85, 95, 96, 104
chi 120, 125
childhood 44, 65
choice 91
choices 82, 83, 90, 91, 92
comfort 113
comfortable 11, 15, 21, 26, 40, 55, 60, 69, 74, 79, 85, 108
conditioning 89
conscientiousness 120
creation 2, 8, 13, 23, 26, 35, 37, 45, 46, 104, 116, 121

D

darkness 29, 32, 120
death 37, 54, 72, 88, 105, 115, 116
delusion 120

127

Dervish 116, 120
detachment 41, 115, 116, 120
diet 19, 82, 84, 90, 124
disciple 66, 120

E

earthwork 105
ecstasy 21
ego 14, 64, 65, 69, 73, 77, 79, 82, 112
Einstein 106
emotion 4, 77
emotions 3, 4, 23, 47, 50, 54, 72, 108, 123
emptiness 32
energy 8, 10, 17, 18, 19, 20, 21, 35, 37, 50, 51, 72, 73, 76, 79, 98, 112, 121, 123, 125
enlightenment 31, 41, 51, 65, 112, 115, 120, 122
entropy 121
evolutionary 124
existence 4, 35, 37, 53, 54, 72, 75, 85, 88, 89, 105, 106, 121

F

failure 37
faith 17, 83, 87, 92
fear 7, 35, 37
forgiveness 52
freedom 7, 9, 40, 41, 73, 74, 85, 88, 114
free will 7, 11, 95, 114
frustration 5, 99

G

God 1, 2, 3, 4, 5, 9, 72, 87, 111, 112
Great Spirit 21, 73, 111, 121
guilt 9
guru 121

H

healing 17, 121
health 20

I

immortality 37
immune system 18, 19
inner chatter 97
inner court 81, 82, 83, 85
inner space 4, 50, 66, 81, 82, 83, 84, 85
intelligence 24, 32, 46, 112, 125
intention 10, 17, 21, 26
interpretation 103, 104

J

jewelry 24
jewels 95
job 8, 10, 37, 43, 73, 81
joy 20, 47, 99, 113

L

language 10, 103
laughter 19, 20, 91, 116
learning 120
life vii, 3, 5, 7, 9, 15, 17, 24, 27, 29, 31, 35, 36, 38, 43, 45, 49, 50, 53, 64, 66, 72, 73, 75, 95, 96, 98, 104, 105, 106, 111, 113, 115, 120
love 5, 8, 9, 17, 54, 77, 83, 124

M

mantra vii, 57, 60
master 44, 51, 65, 67, 87, 88, 113
medicine 19, 20, 83, 98
meditation 11, 15, 21, 26, 30, 32, 47, 52, 55, 60, 69, 74, 79, 85, 93, 100, 107, 108, 111, 122
message 35, 57, 73

mind vii, 2, 5, 8, 13, 19, 21, 23, 31, 32, 35, 38, 40, 44, 45, 47, 49, 54, 55, 59, 60, 63, 64, 65, 67, 77, 82, 83, 85, 89, 90, 97, 105, 106, 115, 122, 123, 124
mindfulness vii, 32, 40, 65, 85
monsters 45

N

nature viii, 25, 30, 45, 49, 72, 81, 89, 93, 95, 99, 100, 104, 115, 121, 122, 123, 124
Nirvana 119
nourishment 4, 59, 88

O

omnipresent 122

P

pain 17, 19, 27, 36, 44
phenomenon 123
practice 8, 32, 51, 55, 59, 64, 65, 82, 84, 98, 114
Present Moment 123
pure action 51, 52
Pure Consciousness 123
pure speech 51
pure thought 51, 52

R

regulate 98
rishi 113
rotate 98, 99
Rumi 4

S

sage 113
self 13, 19, 24, 25, 32, 36, 50, 63, 72, 73, 77, 83, 111, 112, 116, 122

spirit 3, 24, 25, 45, 46, 63, 73, 111, 124
Spiritual Wandering 124
Sufi master 87

T

Tao 112, 124
time 63, 103, 104, 106, 107, 108
timeless 81, 85, 108
transcending 52
transformed 1, 23, 73
transforming 23
true 5, 20, 24, 25, 36, 54, 66, 76, 112, 116, 121, 122, 123, 124
truth 53, 55

U

universe 1, 40, 52, 53, 65, 67, 73, 87, 88, 92, 111, 112, 120

W

willpower 84
wisdom 29, 35, 36, 40, 45, 51, 53, 71, 73, 77, 82, 122, 123
work 5, 10, 19, 35, 43, 59, 78, 83, 96, 103

Y

yoga 13, 19, 49

Z

Zen 44, 65, 67
Zoroaster 51

About the Author

The Messenger had been searching for the meaning and purpose of life since childhood.

The deep and burning questions about life and God caused the Messenger to explore many cultures and traditions for fulfillment.

A new dimension opened when the Messenger was transformed by an extraordinary out-of-body experience.

This book reflects the messages received from that reality.

Made in United States
North Haven, CT
18 April 2023

35562071R00086